# Life Ain't Nice, So Get Over It!

# Life Ain't Nice, So Get Over It!

## Insights to Move You From Stuck To Unstoppable!

### Patrice Baker

iUniverse, Inc.
Bloomington

**LIFE AIN'T NICE, SO GET OVER IT!**
**Insights to Move You From Stuck To Unstoppable!**

*iUniverse books may be ordered through booksellers or by contacting:*

*iUniverse*
*1663 Liberty Drive*
*Bloomington, IN 47403*
*www.iuniverse.com*
*1-800-Authors (1-800-288-4677)*

*ISBN: 978-1-4620-4390-3 (sc)*
*ISBN: 978-1-4620-4391-0 (hc)*
*ISBN: 978-1-4620-4392-7 (ebk)*

*Printed in the United States of America*

*iUniverse rev. date: 08/22/2011*

Dedication

This book is dedicated to the memory of my grandparents
John & Penina Diggs

To the life of my parents
Laron & Mable Diggs Henderson

To my children
Trina Leshay Williams-Johnson
Elijah Edward Baker
In Memoriam: Uvian Charlene Williams

To the future
My granddaughter-Destiny Leshay Doxey

# Acknowledgements

I thank God for placing me in a family of people who planted seeds of faith, education, hard work, and love that make me who I am today. To the memories of those who are no longer here; Laron Henderson (my Dad), Vivian Charlene Williams, Edna Diggs Mahon, Wilma Diggs Hunt, William Pruitt, Eric Laron Henderson, Diana Johnson-Boyd, Linda Bradford-Pace and Phyllis Daniels.

Members of Christ United Presbyterian Church who have embraced my family from the time we arrived in San Diego. Special thanks to: Rev. George Walker Smith & family, Mrs. Ardele Matthews and Mrs. Jean Young, who have always supported my business endeavors.

Spiritual Advisors include: Dr's James & Llouilyn Hargett, Rev. David & Michele Phears, Rev. Arthur Cribbs & Rev. Reginald Gary. To those not mentioned – thank you!

Spiritual & Life Support: I thank God. Thanks to longtime family friend and mentor: Mrs. Vivian "Aunt Viv" Brown. Beverly Coleman: lifelong friend and best bud. Constance Smith, Dorothy Richards and Elisa Cullaty: you have inspired and support me in ways that cannot be measured. Special thanks to Ambrose Brodus. You are priceless and I love you all.

Special Thanks: Carolyn Y. Smith and Elisa Cullaty for guiding my words through the process.

To those of you who said to me, I can't wait until you write your book. Thank You for seeing something in me that I did not see in myself.

# Contents

# Why I Wrote This Book

My reason for writing this book is twofold: 1) to honor my grandparents and acknowledge how their seeds continue to sprout in their children, grandchildren and on through the family line and 2) to let women know that when you feel stuck, frustrated, unhappy, overwhelmed or faced with what seems like insurmountable odds—that you are not alone. As a good friend once told me, HELP is on the way! Regardless of what you might think, you can create the space within yourself to receive all that you desire and deserve. You must believe that you can, have a willing spirit and recognize that God's Amazing Grace is active your life. My grandparents did and so can you.

## John & Penina Diggs—my Grandparents

> *"Issac sowed seed in that land, and in the same year reaped a hundredfold. The Lord blessed him"*

> *Genesis 26.12.*

A famous Televangelist used Genesis 26:12 as the basis for his message on how we ought to handle tough times in our lives. He said that when we are in the most need; whether it is a need for money, a job, a home, good health or whatever, that instead of being *need* oriented, we ought to become *seed oriented*—and give away the very thing that we need in order to be a blessings to someone else. I don't know about you but that didn't make sense to me. However, as I continued to listen to the message I began to think of it from another perspective—what my ancestors might have thought about that.

You see, my family and I were in the process of planning our family reunion and my grandparents were already in my thoughts.

So, I connected the seeds, if you will. Back to the time when my grandparents had to feed, clothe, care for and instill family values in my mother and her 9 siblings. Sowing these seeds with the faith that their children would have a better life, whether they lived to see the fruits of their labor or not. To sow means "to set something in motion" and that is what they did. Despite having to face the challenge of working the soil—a soil hardened by racism, discrimination and hatred for black people—simply because of the color of their skin. With no guarantee that the seeds they sowed would ever take root, my grandparents, John and Pennina Diggs took what they believed to be true and began to plant seeds.

## Arkansas 1880-1930

They were sharecroppers in Arkansas, after the end of the Civil War, responsible for raising their 10 children—"the amount of land allocated to the sharecropper was determined by the number of productive laborers within the family. People resisted the harsh condition in which they were forced to live and work. To make the sharecropping system work, violence in the form of *lynching was frequently used. Between 1889 and 1918 there was 214 known lynching in the Arkansas. In this thirty-five year period, 182 of the victims, or 85% were black. Five of the 182 were black women. Ninety-three, or 43% of the 214 victims were black residents of the Delta. Of the ten states that had more than 100 lynching, Arkansas ranked sixth after Georgia, Mississippi, Texas, Louisiana, and Alabama. By 1927, the number of lynchings had reached 313."

Taken from The Sharecropping System—an article written by
Norman Vickers

*"Lynching Statistics—Throughout the late 19th Century racial tension grew throughout the United States. More of this tension was noticeable in the Southern parts of the United States. In the south, people were blaming their financial problems on the newly freed slaves that lived around them. Lynchings (hanging people) were becoming a popular way of resolving some of the anger that whites had in relation to the free blacks.

From 1882-1968, 4,743 lynchings occurred in the United States. Of these people that were lynched 3,446 were black . . . . Out of the 4,743 . . . only 1,297 while people were lynched. Many of the whites were lynched for helping blacks or being anti-lynching and even for domestic crimes.

Most of the lynchings that took place happened in the South. A big reason for this was the end of the Civil War. Once blacks were given their freedom, many people felt that the freed blacks were getting away with too much freedom and felt that they needed to be controlled."

Lynching Statistics for 1882-1968 faculty.berea.edu/browners/
chesnutt/classroom/lynchingstat.html

Historic Documents confirm the horrific conditions that many Blacks endured well after the end of the Civil War. This was a time when all Americans were supposed to be free. It was very tough and many did not make it. Those who survived relied on their faith, perseverance and love.

## The Seeds They Planted

John and Pennina Diggs were born in Morrilton, Arkansas in 1875 & 1884 respectively. They had a solid foundation in the church and understood that it was their faith and the faith of their forefathers that brought them through otherwise devastating circumstances. The seeds they planted were based on the very things that they wanted their children to have and to carry forward—values based on hard work, education, faith, respect for others and family love. When they encountered tough times, as they often did, they didn't complain—they just went to work.

My Grandparents were an integral part of the African Methodist Episcopal (AME) Zion Church, where my grandfather served as a deacon. My grandmother, you might say, helped hold the church together financially, as she was the person the church relied on to continually prepare the budget. In fact, my grandmother would take the 'twins', (my mother Mable and her sister Marie) with her when she accompanied the Pastor to the Annual Conference to make the financial report. She always had the most money to report, making sure all dues were paid and everything was in order. Although the odds seemed insurmountable, she stayed focused on what had to be done—doing what she could. Her fundraising efforts involved her children as well, especially the 'twins' who were the youngest girls.

My grandmother was a very giving woman. She would sew for anyone who was in need—she once took a quilt and made a coat for a little girl who didn't have one and when a man asked her to make a tent for him, she did. When visiting Ministers and the Bishop came to town, they always stayed at my Grandparents home and enjoyed the Southern hospitality of good food and a warm bed.

My mother remembers how when she was very young, my grandmother would make ice cream and she and her sister would take it into town and sell it from the store porch every Saturday for 10 cents a bowl. She said, it was amazing how far that ice cream went. I believe that was the training ground for developing my Mom's sales skills because anyone who knows her says, "Mable can sell ice water to Eskimos". She has carried on the tradition in helping to raise funds for her church, her Sorority, Alpha Kappa Alpha (AKA) and a variety of other organizations and groups that work to help the community.

**When they encountered tough times, as they often did, they didn't complain—they just went to work**. This becomes a familiar theme that appears throughout the book and is one of the seeds planted by my Grandparents that continues to sprout in our family, even today.

I must admit, that when I sat down to write this book, this was not the book I had planned to write. Believe me, I know exactly where my blessings have come from and I am convinced without a doubt that God is the source—it's just that I didn't feel qualified to speak from that platform. My walk is not based on any biblical credential or Seminary training—that has not been my foundation. However, it *is* based on the foundation of being raised in the church; singing in the choir, attending bible study as a child and as an adult, attending several churches in my search to find the "right one", taking a time-out from church and then being pulled back in by the Holy Spirit. I once heard a writer say, that he didn't write the book, the book wrote him and I wondered what he was talking about. Now I know. This book has written itself, all I had to do was get out of the way.

# Chapter 1

## Everybody's Got One, So What's Your Story Got To Do With Anything?

*Who can find a virtuous woman? For her worth is far above rubies.*

*Proverbs 31:10*

I can still hear her words ringing in my ears, "Patrice, *Seek Ye First the Kingdom of Heaven*!". I was talking to a dear friend of mind, Diana, and she was listening to yet another story of my awkward attempt at loving someone who didn't love me back. Not in the way I wanted or needed to be loved anyway. And she would always respond to me in the same loving way with these same loving words—Seek Ye First the Kingdom of Heaven. At that time, I really didn't know what she was talking about—so I just listened. You know how it is when you recognize you're getting seeds of wisdom, but, you have no idea what it means, so you just smile or nod. Luckily our conversations were always on the phone, so she couldn't see my face. You see, that is not what I wanted to hear. I wanted an answer to my problem or rather a way to get that person to love me, in spite of all the red lights, warnings signals and danger signs posted in plain sight—I would not be deterred from my mission.

How does that happen? After all, I was not a child. I was a grown woman who held down a full time job, took care of my children, was smart and resourceful and on and on. I had even been married once or twice . . . Anyway, I was the one other people called for advice about love, life and whatever else—so I must know something. I was on a mission and I had **my story** and I was sticking to it. And my story, just like your story was propelling me full steam ahead in my search for love and happiness. I thought that's all there was to it, just keep moving ahead. I didn't realize that what had happened to me so far was just the prelude to the opening dance of my life.

You see, our stories have everything to do with it; with our life decisions and choices, our fears and beliefs about ourselves and other people, and even our ability to see and activate the power that lies within. What I didn't know is there *was* and *is more* to the story.

## *My original story:*

It started on November 3rd in the year that I was born in Little Rock (Pulaski County), Arkansas. At that time it was just me—I am the oldest child—and as you know from the story about my ancestors (and history) we lived in a tough part of the world for people of color. In 1956 when my family moved to California (thank you Jesus!) our family had grown to include my sister Barbara and my Mom was pregnant with my younger sister, Angela. In 1959, my brother Eric was born.

This is where my story began—with my Dad and me.

Have you ever had a relationship that existed only in your mind? The people may be real, but the actual relationship between the two of you is a figment of your own imagination? It may have been between you and someone you wanted to be like, or a teacher you admired, or as in my case, a parent. You see, my Dad died when I was nine years old. You would think that in nine years, my Dad and I would have plenty of opportunities to bond, as father and daughter. And in most cases, you would probably be right. But in my case, it didn't happen.

I grew up in a home with a father and mother who accepted and understood the responsibility in caring for us—their children. We had food on the table, a roof over our heads and clothes to wear. It wasn't until I became an adult, when my Mom and I were having a conversation that she told me, at one point after my Dad died, we were poor. Well, I was surprised, as were my siblings when I told them later, because we all felt so secure, so taken care of that we didn't *feel* poor.

As the oldest of four children, I naturally gravitated toward the lead role of peacemaker in the family (I was a mediator in training). I appeared strong, capable, responsible, and I was able to speak on behalf of others without any emotional attachment to the outcome. So, that was my role and it seemed to be working. Except for the fact that inside, emotionally I was two years old, everything else was fine.

## Stopped

Looking back, I realize that I created this story in my mind about the relationship between my Dad and me using a scenario I was comfortable with. As a child I loved to watch westerns on my family's black and white television set. The Rifleman was one of my favorites. You see, I am a cowgirl at heart, and I envisioned that from the time I was born, my Dad and me stood on opposite sides of some imaginary line. We had what is called a "stalemate" in our relationship and we stood there facing one another, with our hands on our six-shooters, daring the other to cross that invisible line. *(Remember, this is from the mind of a child during the fifties)*. Neither one of us realized that if we took a few steps toward the other person, opened our arms and our minds, that our hearts might be opened also. But, as I said before, that did not happen.

After my Dad died, it took a while for the anger to rise to the surface and raise its ugly head. I was nine years old and if I ever needed a Dad, it was then. *How else would I learn how to have healthy relationships with men?* At first, I pretended that everything was okay. Being the capable, bright young lady that I was—the loss did not appear to be so bad—*you know they didn't talk about stuff like that then*—*especially to children*—the adults knew best and I would be okay. So, I played the role of protector for everyone else; I had become the spokesperson for those in need of a strong voice and I ignored and covered up the emotional hole that was growing inside of me.

As you can imagine, I was **not** okay! My feelings of abandonment turned into hurt, the hurt turned into fear and the fear turned into **anger.** I was mad. I had spent a great deal of time trying to have everybody else's back—and nobody had mine! The more I played the role of speaking up for others, the less I spoke up for myself. I would hear people say, *Patrice is so strong, she can handle it.* The truth is, I wasn't handling it. I was faking it. For most of my adult life, I carried around the anger and nagging pain of being emotionally **stopped.** That is how I see it now. I was stopped emotionally because I was still waiting for my Dad to show up.

I carried this anger into my relationships, especially with men. No matter how open I appeared to be, I never allowed anyone to get to know the real me. I knew that under that strong veneer was an angry, insecure, scared little girl. What I didn't know then, was that beneath my fears and anger was a beautiful, loving and lovable woman—who is enough—waiting to be set free (more in Chapter 3). And the strange thing is that the very thing I longed to have—a man to care for and watch out for me—was the very thing that I denied myself access to. I would retreat to the safety of my western movie, hands on my six-shooter, daring anyone to cross that invisible line.

The anger I felt seeped into my relationship with my Mom, because at one point, I blamed her. Crazy as it seems now, I blamed her for not ensuring that I had a relationship with my Dad before he died. I thought it was her job to know what I needed from my Dad and to ensure I got it. I didn't understand until later, that she was struggling with her own feelings of loss, pain and probably anger. After all, she lost a husband and the father of her children. As I understand it now, it was her strength, love and commitment to us that kept us shielded from potential poverty or worse. But, at the time, it was all about me.

When I had my own children, I carried the strength, love and commitment that I got from my Mom and passed it on to them. I also carried the anger. And as people often say, God don't like ugly! My first two children were beautiful, brilliant girls and my third child was a beautiful boy. (I wasn't prepared to see boys as brilliant . . . yet). I thought this is good; two daughters and a son. As my son was growing up, my ugly stayed hidden because he was a cute baby and a handsome little boy. It wasn't until one day I realized I was looking into the eyes of a young man. Physically, mentally and psychologically, my handsome little boy was becoming a man. I thought, how did this happen? It is amazing what happens when you aren't paying attention.

I thought, here we go again. I am reminded of the very thing that I had missed all of my life (a relationship with my main man—Dad) and that reminder is standing in my house! So, I went into my closet of shame and pulled out my baggage labeled Dad MIA (missing in action), and I became angry all over again. I was angry because I had missed out on having that special relationship with my Dad—where he would hold me in his arms and tell me everything would be okay and teach me how to look out for myself in relationships with men. You see, my memories of him are gone. It's as if the event of his death were so traumatic for me—the feeling of loss so profound that I lost the ability to recover that part of my life.

Whatever it was, the fact that my son was becoming a man served as a trigger, reminding me of the anger I had tried all my life to hide. In that moment, I realized that I could not escape my past any longer, because my past was somehow, connected to my future. My ability to start the healing process was directly connected to the opportunity to live a happy, healthy, spirit driven life. And another thing, this was my child, not my father. And I had to get over it!

## Get over it!

Don't get me wrong! *Getting over it!* ain't easy or simple—and does not happen overnight. Getting over the emotional void, pain and damage done to our hearts and minds (either real or imagined) is a long, tough, even painful process by itself, and can seem to last a lifetime. I feel like I have had several lifetimes.

That being said, I chose to do the work necessary to *get over it*, because of my son. (I know that God does have a sense of humor). Especially when I realized that the same awkwardness I felt with men was showing up in my relationship with my son.

The hardest part of my journey was that even after some good counseling sessions, sharing my feelings with those closest to me, and sharing some of my pain with my Mom (and hearing some of hers), and even after lots of conversations with God, the one person that I wanted to, needed to talk to, was my Dad. But, I couldn't—he was gone. And for me, that opportunity was no longer available.

Even when I made the choice to heal, it was difficult. I have been blinded by pain for so long, that it was hard to imagine what I had to do to even approach the wall I had built around me, to the love, especially to the part where I was able to love myself first. God had answered my prayers in an unexpected way. It is *because* I had a son that I made the decision to face my issues and start the healing process. What I know now is that a large part of who I am and why I am here is directly related to my Dad.

## Unstoppable

Part of the healing process, for me, has been acceptance. I had to learn to accept *what was, and what is,* in spite of, how *I* wanted it to be. Isn't that how God loves us, in spite of ourselves? That was probably the hardest thing for me to do. To accept my past, without getting the answers to my heartfelt questions about what it really felt like to have a Dad in my life. Instead I chose to move forward, in spite of it all—ya'll know that ain't easy. I have come to realize that the healing ain't over. My goal is not to get to the end of my healing—my goal is to always **remember** that no matter how long I live, I am *always* in the process of healing something.

Thinking about my Dad now, I wish I knew more about him. I wish I knew more about his pain, his joys and his goals in life. You see, knowing what is happening on the inside of another person enables us to make that connection—to see them as human, just like us. I was so busy thinking about what I had missed, that I forgot about how he might have felt about his life. I may have come to understand sooner that my Dad was not a mind reader, he was a man; that he didn't choose to leave me, he died; and that maybe there were many things he would have shared with me, if he had the chance. There is so much, I have learned, about what we don't know. Yet, we continue to make decisions based on faulty or incomplete information. Just as I didn't know that my beautiful son would one day have his own pain and anger as a teenager, growing up in a world among men greatly in need of the wisdom and the loving embrace of their Dad, in a world that is not always user friendly to people of color.

Now, when I think about my Dad and me, I think about the possibility. Not so much of what could have been, but of what is and what can be for me. He and I are part of the same legacy. The legacy of hard work, family values, faith, fellowship and love that came through our ancestors to each of us. I had a choice. I could either remain on **stop**—stuck in my past, blind to the real issues, blaming my Dad or I could create the space to receive and embrace all that God has for me, and become **unstoppable.** It came to me that every time I repeated my own cycle of pain and held someone else hostage in it, that I had to remain close to make sure they couldn't get away. Therefore, I was being held hostage as well. In the end, the events of my life did not change, they happened just as I remembered them. What did change was how I chose to respond to the events called my life, and how my response helped to shape my relationship with the most influential people in my life—between my Dad, my Mom and me.

*Food for thought: Can YOU make a difference in a child's life?*

For those with children, grandchildren, other people's children, or remember how it was to be a child, I have several questions for you. What do the children who show up in your life, say about you? Do they know how you feel about them? Do they see the love that you have to offer? Do you have love to offer? Do they see your love as unconditional (no matter what) or are there stipulations and conditions associated with your ability to give and receive love? Is your love metered out based on performance, accomplishments or how well they do on a test. I understand the desire to want them to do their best and be their best, however, in that effort, do we sometime lose sight of them as human beings.

Do you ask the children you come into contact with how they *feel* about the events in their lives and in the world? Even when you ask them questions, are you patient enough to hear their answers? Do you notice that when they are unable to give an answer, that many of our children are mad and angry themselves?

And what does that mean to you? It means that you have to find a way to get close; to figure out how to walk with them and beside them without questions or ulterior motives—and learn to just *be*. At some point, when they become adults, you will be a part of their story. So, when they look back on their lives, what will they say they needed from us—and didn't get. What will be said or written about you. What are the possibilities you can create for those *young, angry, confused, searching minds?* Will it be acceptable to say you didn't know how to reach them? Will they buy that? Do you? Just as I said before, it all comes back around. It is all connected.

*Starting today:*

The truth is that not everyone believes that they have something to offer another person. There are so many distractions in the world that it is easy to get caught up; in the latest trends and technology, and lose sight of the brilliance and value you bring to the world. I know that people do business, and spend time with, people they like and that in order to truly love yourself, you have to like yourself first.

What I know for sure is that children have a sense for the truth. We, as adults, are like a case study in life and they become experts by observation. Children make a direct connection to the truth based on what you say and what you do. When they make the observation that your walk is not consistent with your talk, to them, it looks like a lie. They don't know or even care about the backstory, after all they weren't there. They need the best you have to offer and if, for whatever reason, you don't like yourself, it will show up instead.

What I am suggesting is that you may be showing behavior based on negative experiences, things not yet achieved, regret or self-hatred without knowing it. Because at the end of the day, we all have the tendency to think about all the stuff we have left to do, rather then what we have accomplished.

For one week, I want you to think about what you like about you. Carry a notepad around so that whenever something comes to mind, you can write it down. You can also ask other people (who you know like you) what *they* like about you, as well, however, it is important that you accept what they say. This is not a debate. This is designed to help you *remember* what is already likeable about you and to use your likeable qualities to make a difference in the lives of our children.

Here are some attributes to get you started:

## What I like about me—Likeable Qualities

My smile
Personality
Resilience
Creativity
Tenacity
Caring spirit
Desire to help people
Ability to connect easily with people
Adventurous nature
Sense of humor
Life-long learner
Approachable
Did I mention fun!

My body (just as it is)

I believe you will be amazed at how much you have inside of you to give to that fatherless child, who may be waiting just for you.

# Chapter 2

## Can You Pass The Sanity Test?

For you have need or **endurance,** so that after you *have*
done the will of God, you may receive the promise:
*For yet a little while and He who is coming will come*
*and will not tarry. Now the just shall live by faith; but if*
*anyone draws back, My soul has no pleasure in him*

Hebrews10: 36-38

*Word wealth: endurance.* Constancy, perseverance, continuance, patient endurance . . . the capacity to continue to bear up under difficult circumstances, not with a passive complacency, but with a hopeful fortitude that actively resists weariness and defeat.

According to Albert Einstein, a man considered to be a genius even today, the definition of insanity is to do the same thing over and over again and to expect a different result. Well, there it is. I have failed the sanity test. For some of us, that definition is a way of life. Anyone who's broken a habit knows how difficult that can be—let alone changing a lifestyle. In that regard, those of us who like to stay in our comfort zones or attempt to remain under the radar in order to avoid the challenges of life; or who believe that if I am a nice person, life will be nice to me. To that I say, life aint' nice, so get over it!

### I'm a Mom

Life offers many opportunities for us to question the "sanity" of our lives. Not only when things don't go the way we want them to, but, on a deeper level when we begin to question the meaning of our lives. Those kinds of questions can make you go deep within yourself where you come face to face with the truth of what you truly believe; to the core of who you are and of what you perceive your purpose to be. I have been there. Where the very core of everything I believed to be true or understood about life was in question. It is not a place for the faint of heart. Oh, and don't go in alone.

This is the hardest part of the book for me to write. In my effort to share my story and to possibly help somebody else, I have to convey an emotional side of my experience that I have never quite come to grips with. Questions like, why did I respond the way I did in times of crisis? What made me tell God that I wanted to see what was going on with my son? How was I able to move forward and deal with this situation on a day by day, event by event basis, without being paralyzed by the very thought of what was really going on?

I remember the determination that I felt and the clarity I had in regards to the mission. The mission was to keep my son from becoming a statistic. Yet, I never allowed myself to sit in the realization that this was so beyond anything that I have ever had to do, that it was truly a super natural experience. And I believe that God gave me the strength and guidance to go into a super natural state to deal with it. And once again, w*hen they encountered tough times, as they often did, they didn't complain—they just went to work.* So, here goes.

## Stopped

By the time my son turned sixteen, my daughter was a young woman on her own (they are 12 years apart) and I was once again a single parent. I remember returning home from work or the store and on several occasions finding a specific group of items, in a circle on the living room floor. At the top of the circle was the big family bible, two of my ceramic items on the sides and a kitchen knife at the bottom of the circle. They would be placed together in front of the sofa or the love seat wherever my son had been sitting. And since it was just he and I and I know I didn't put them there, I asked him what it was and said I thought it looked like a ritual. His response would be, "no, it's not a ritual"—but, I kept thinking—looks like a ritual to me. Even though I had noticed this as somewhat of a pattern, it took a while for me to make the connection that there might be a problem.

Now there were other things going on as well. He was having difficulty in school, not only with his grades, but, also in his behavior. He was getting into fights with other boys and no matter how much I probed or tried to find out what was wrong, he would say that I was overreacting, that I was creating the problem and to just leave him alone. I must admit at that time in my life, I believed that my ability to be a good parent was directly related to how much fear I instilled in my children. I use the word fear loosely—meaning it was my way of maintaining control and order in my home. The kind of fear associated with them doing the right thing—a fear of God or not being approved by God kind of thing.

As a single parent, I needed all the leverage that I could get. I was not helpless by any means, however, I knew a good line when I heard one and was not shy about quoting Bill Cosby as often as needed, *I brought you into this world, and I will take you out!* Not always the best strategy when the goal is to have open communication with a teenager, but, it worked—usually.

This was different and I knew one thing for sure. My son is a good person. And something else had to be going on. So, I did something that would change my life forever. I asked God to let me *see* what was really going on. I remember that day very clearly. I had gotten angry with my son over something and I was so angry & frustrated with him because he wouldn't answer my questions that I was probably a little out of control. Okay, yes, I was out of control. Then suddenly, I **stopped.** I looked at my son and as if I were seeing him for the first time—and I realized **he was not the enemy.** In that moment, I just turned and walked out of his room. As I walked down the hallway, I said to God, I want to see what is happening with my child.

And with those words, our world changed.

Let me take you back to that walk down the hallway to my seemingly simple, yet world shattering request. Some would say that I wasn't in my right mind (insanity) when I said I wanted to see the truth. Because that is what I was really asking—to see the truth about what was going on inside of my son. The parts I couldn't see, as a mother, therefore if I couldn't see inside of him—I would not be able to protect, or fight or **deal with** whatever was causing him to change before my eyes. And this was happening in my home, on my turf! Maybe that control thing was taking over; or it was the voice of my ancestors ringing in my ears, or it could have been that I was a fatherless child with a strong mother who learned early in life how to fight for others. Whatever the reason, I didn't stop to think what would happen next. I went to the only source I knew who had the answer that I needed—and it was one of the best things I have ever done in my life.

I will not give you a blow-by-blow account of events in my life after that night. My desire is allow you to see what was happening from an inside point of view. Mine. There is always more than one side, perspective or viewpoint to any story and, of course, my son has his. However, in an effort to tell you a little about me, you may also see glimpses of my son and his genius.

## *My mind was made up!*

Yes, I was forced to make a decision and my mind was made up. I was **going** to take my son in for a psychiatric evaluation. Don't ask me how I planned to do it. Actually, I didn't have a plan. This journey, for me, has not been about planning, it is more about what happens when **intention** meets a **made up mind** under the **direction of God** through **His amazing Grace**. After a while, I began to tell people that I had seen Grace and it was alive and well, walking around in the body of a 180lb, 6'1" black man—whom I call my son. That's my truth, and I'm sticking to it.

You see, just a year or so before this happened, I had gone through a very dark, uncertain time in my life. And because I am a problem solver by nature, I sought the help of professionals (therapists) to help me get through it. I see now that my decision to take care of myself directly impacted my ability to be fully present and to be a partner in helping my son through his dark days. I believe I had been prepared for this moment in time. This is one of the numerous times when focused intention to help my son (in spite of himself), a made up mind and the divine hand of God's grace worked together in my life.

## *Get Over it!*

I made an appointment at Kaiser. I was taking my son in for an evaluation in the morning. When I arrived home from work that evening, it was late and the house was dark. My son was usually home and so I didn't know what to think. While I was trying to figure out who to call, the phone rang. It was a police officer and he asked me to identify my son by name, which I did. Then a strange thing happened, the officer paused and in a hesitant voice asked, *is he alright?* And in a similar hesitant voice, I responded, *I don't think so, why.* He said that my son would open his mouth and nothing would come out, but it was clear that he was being distracted by something internal. Although I had scheduled the appointment with Kaiser, I asked the officer, in my most humble voice, "Can you keep him and have him checked out". Even though I knew the answer would be no, my heart sank just a little when I heard the word. The officer said they had given my son something to eat and that I could pick him up anytime to take him home. It was a minor incident and he probably wouldn't be charged. Truthfully, I didn't want to pick him up because I wasn't sure *who* I would be bringing home.

On the way home, my son continued to be distracted by something internal, although in a moment of clarity, he did agree that something was wrong—then he later denied it. For a long time this was our model for communication; moments of clarity, agree or acknowledge, then deny—otherwise deny, deny, deny.

It was obvious to me, from the start that I had to stay alert, attentive and observant of what was happening, as well as, listen for what was not being said. In the initial consultation, my son was not very talkative and the Doctor although he was talking to him, he was not looking at him—but, I was. So, when the Doctor asked him, *do you hear voices,* his first response was, *nah.* When I realized the Doctor was going on to the next question, I spoke up and said, wait a minute and I asked my son, if you heard voices, would you tell us, he answered, *nah* and then said, *yeah, I hear voices.* Immediately, the Doctor looked up and said, I'll be right back. And with that, life took on a whole new meaning.

## Signs of things to come

From the start, I had to pay close attention to my son's facial expressions, because, when a person is experiencing internal messages or prompts from the inside, it often shows on their face. In an instant a smile could turn to a frown and his eyes would grow dark with suspicion for no apparent reason. Or he would glance repeated in a specific direction, although there was no one there. I also had to become aware of the amount of physical space between us, before I stepped into his personal space. Previously, I didn't have to think about it. I would step into both my children's personal space when I felt like I needed to. Being a strong black mom may have something to do with that. However, it became clear that behavior had to change.

Other things had changed as well—these were different times.

I didn't have to be so concerned with my own facial reactions to what was happening, because I had developed the ability to appear stoic under stressful, uncertain and scary times. And this situation was certainly qualified as such. The clique, *never let them see you sweat* turned into *never let them see you scared* for me. Because, when all was said and done, I was the one person that stood between my son and the entire medical/mental health system and all the associated organizations, and if I fell down, so would he. I was clear about that and I took the responsibility and my own well-being seriously.

Being fair, I must make an attempt to give you a glimpse of the other side; or as a good friend of mine often refers to as *the dark side.* For the sake of my child, I had to go to the places where he had to go and be open to hear some of what he was being told, on the inside. I've had to cross a few lines (by calling 911) and appear to betray his confidence and risk losing him to a force that I couldn't see. The fact that I had to share personal experiences and my observations of his changes in behavior to medical personnel was, at one time, considered as a betrayal. I had to risk looking like the enemy in the eyes of my son.

And just like any recovering co-dependent, I had to learn to back off. You see, as his life was changing, so was mine. Today, we have a bond and the best relationship I can hope to have with a child of mine; in fact, with both my children and my granddaughter. In letting go of the feelings associated with betrayal, self-hatred and judgment, we have experienced some generational healing together.

## *Unstoppable*

**Disclaimer: The following action should only be taken when within your spirit you believe that you have no other choice. And then don't ever stop praying.**

What I know (and knew at the time), is that when we are in need of help, we are told in an emergency, when lives are at stake, to call the police. I knew I couldn't call family and friends, unless I had something specific for them to do, although, there were times when family and friends did help. On those occasions, when I needed my son taken to the facility where I knew he would get immediate help, rather than, ending up as a casualty in jail or in the morgue (from my perspective, those were the only other choices) I did what I had to do. I called the San Diego Police Department (SDPD). I needed them to protect and serve. Aligned in prayer with God I had to take things second by second. I didn't have the luxury of seeing ahead or second guessing what I ought to do. I just knew what I had to do. And for me, it worked every time.

When they showed up, I would explain why, according to *code 5150, this was an emergency and where exactly I wanted them to take my son. At first, when he was still a minor, and later when I was his Conservator, the name Mesa Vista Hospital would roll off of my tongue. Another thing, no matter where you want your loved one taken, that last thing you want to happen is for the police to leave without them. From that point on, your credibility may forever be in question because, after all, you are the adult who keeps saying you know what is best. Again, I didn't have time to think about that, I had to stay focused on the targeted end result.

*\*Section 5150 is a section of the California Welfare and Institutions Code which allows a qualified officer or clinician to involuntarily confine a person deemed to have a mental disorder that makes them a danger to him or her self and/or others and/or is gravely disabled.*

*Some symptoms may be prolonged lack of sleep, not eating or taking care of personal hygiene or outbursts of unprovoked anger. Non-attentive or non-responsiveness due to internal stimulation or conversations with someone you can't see.*

Anyone who has received a medical or mental health diagnosis knows that our wonderful medical health industry has its flaws. The fact that they are all human is the common thread that runs between them all, and also through you. Therefore, there is no single entity on earth that has the answer or the cure for you or your loved one. Often, the *right* medication is found due to trial and error. You try it and if you don't have too many side effects or life threatening symptoms and it works, then there it is. The unfortunate reality is that medication can only do so much and even in the trial and error period, things are going to happen.

Relapse in real terms occurs when a person decides that they feel better and no longer need the very medication that has helped them to feel good in the first place. Or, if a person returns to a negative behavior or habit that puts them in harm or danger. We get into trouble when our expectation is that the miracle of healing is going to happen the first time, or the second time, or *ever*. The truth is that there are problems and conditions in life that can never be solved.

And, it is our faith in something other than ourselves that allows us to wake up each day and say, yes! I want to be here.

I remember where I was when after 2 or 3 (or maybe more) of my son's relapses, the truth of what was happening finally hit me. I got it! I was standing in my bedroom. I had just spoken to one of the doctors where my son had been hospitalized (again). I just stood there all alone. I remember being amazed that this was continuing to happen one more time—and in that moment, I realized my mistake. My misguided thinking that this would be over soon, or ever, was replaced with the reality that this was a lifelong commitment. I didn't think about it long, and maybe that is what has helped me through all of this.

Those seeds planted by my grandparents, w*hen they encountered tough times, as they often did, they didn't complain—they just went to work.*

When we (my son and I) received the initial diagnosis, my question was not, why me? It was, okay Lord, what do I do now? It doesn't mean I was ready to believe it, it just meant I recognized we had a problem. So, on that day, as the truth of that diagnosis finally hit me, I made a silent vow that I would do whatever I had to do to help my son, by any means necessary.

## *Angels everywhere*

When I would get calls at work that meant I had to get up and leave, no questions asked. God has already blessed me with a supervisor who said to me, go, do what you have to do. (Years later, I saw her in the grocery store and I told her how much that meant to me). After getting the call I would go into the restroom (this became my ritual) before I left the building. I would sit in the stall and from the depths of my soul, I would say these words, *I don't know what to do.* What I found out is that those powerful, heartfelt words were exactly what God wanted to hear—because, each and every time, He had already taken care of it. And that is what has enabled me to walk, step by step, through this experience and keep smiling.

From the outside, no one knew what I was going through unless I told them. And that's the thing—I told people. I told the people in my church; people whom I met in the grocery store and in the mall. I told a dear friend in my office, a few people in upper management, friends and family and anyone else I felt led to share it with.

And guess what I found out! I discovered that this was one of the best kept secrets of all times! Each and every time, the response to me was and still is this: I have someone in my family or I have two people in my family or I know someone who is diagnosed . . . Some even referred to back in the days when we had a relative in the back room, who everyone knew was just a little off, or a neighbor or so-and-so down the street. That was both amazing and troubling to me! I wondered how something that affects lives so drastically was not being talked about. I thought about how many people must be suffering in silence.

As far as I know, those people whom I shared parts of my story with didn't talk behind my back. There was no need to. I was looking for help, not gossiping. In fact, when I would see these people again, they would always ask how my son was doing. And when I brought him to church, they would come up to him to give him a hug and share words of encouragement.

That helped me to realize that no matter where I go, I am connected to other people through our human experience. As much as we are different, in our preferences and varied interests, we are connected by life experiences available to each of us.

## Unstoppable

As you can imagine, my decision making ability had to be altered. I could no longer rely on what I knew to be true or what I had done in the past, because I had never dealt with anything like this before. However, the fact that I had to rely on my faith in God was the one thing I knew for sure. I call the series of event that happened next (and continue to happen)—miracles.

*Just 3 of many . . .*

## *Miracle #1*

It was a Sunday night and my son had gone out earlier. I lay in bed trying, without success, to go to sleep. Usually he would be home by now and so my mind was racing with worry. What if he was in jail, or somewhere hurt or dead or was lost and didn't know where he was or had hurt someone else or was with the wrong people or was . . . My mind was racing.

When I couldn't sleep or stop my mind from worrying I would repeat 2 Timothy 1:7 over and over again and I could eventually fall asleep. *"For God has not given us a spirit of fear, but of power and of love and of a **sound mind**."* I had written it on a card and posted it to the wall in my bedroom so that when I looked up I would see it.

As human beings we have choices. Regardless of what we know to be true, we have the ability to choose *when* and *how* to use the resources available to us. And I was no different. I knew what my first line of defense ought to be, but, through my own stubbornness, I chose it last. I was too busy worrying—have you ever been there? There can appear to be comfort in worrying because when you think the worst, you can't be disappointed. It takes conscious effort to stop worrying and to shift your mind into a place of hope and expectancy for the best and to risk the pain felt if you don't get what you pray for. I get that now.

So, when I became sick and tired of worrying I looked up—both to the scripture and to God and then I fell asleep. The next morning I got up and went to work. There was added stress, of course, because I didn't know where my son was—but I did my job and somehow managed to turn off my mind. I felt like I was in a daze—and for some reason I didn't report him missing right away. I got through the day and another night and on Tuesday after I went to work, I filed a missing person report. I met the officer outside of my office building and gave him a description and a picture of my son. We talked briefly after he took my report and let me know that he believed in the power of prayer. This was another confirmation that God always sends the right people.

When I went back into my office, I felt better. A short time later I got a phone call from one of my son's friends. He said that his wife's cousin called to say that my son was at her house waiting for him. Since he hadn't made any arrangement to meet my son, he knew something was wrong and so he called me. When I picked up my son (I could tell that he had been out on the streets) I told him I was taking him home so he could get cleaned up and get something to eat. Although he didn't say much, it was clear that he was distracted and he kept looking around suspiciously.

When we got home and were walking toward the door, he stopped, turned around and started to walk up the street. I called him to come back but he kept walking, so after a while, I went back into the house. I called to amend the missing report and then I turned my conversation to God. Like many other times before, I said, *Okay Lord, I got him to the house, you have to get him to the hospital.* You see, my understanding of how this relationship worked was that I had to do my part—all I knew to do—and then turn it over to God, who always did His part. In fact, that is still my understanding today.

Later that evening, I was scheduled to attend a Council meeting at my church and I had to give a report. Thinking I wouldn't be able to make it, I called my daughter to have her take it for me. I also called a good friend, a Minister who lives in Apple Valley and shared my fear with him. He reminded me that, no matter what, God is still in control and he prayed with me. His words were comforting and soothing to my soul and helped me to be okay, in that moment.

When my daughter came to get the report, I was still typing it. The phone rang and it was a doctor from County Mental Health asking me to confirm my son by name and to tell me that he was okay. This time I was delighted to do so and notified him that I had private insurance coverage. I called my provider and was told that the doctor would have to call them directly this time. A little bit later, I received a call from the doctor saying that my son was on his way to Mesa Vista Hospital. My daughter and I said, *thank you, Lord*, I finished the report and took it myself.

## Miracle #2

When you are going through uncertain times, you are often subjected to the opinions, ideas, attitudes and suggestions of other people. In those circumstances it is very important to know what needs to be done, how it needs to be done and who is able to get it done for you. We have many examples, both in scripture and in life, where people who mean well have plenty of opinions, yet, don't have a clue how to help you. It is imperative to be able to separate the two.

While visiting my son in the hospital, I met a woman whose son had the same diagnosis. We began talking on the phone, sharing our experiences and providing support for one another. On this day I had called the SDPD and I was frustrated because I wasn't getting the response that I wanted—my son didn't appear symptomatic. That happens doesn't it? When your loved one becomes an expert at looking like they don't need help or that nothing is wrong. Anyway, my new support buddy called and asked if I wanted her to come over and I said yes.

Now, I had been through this many times before by myself and I knew what I had to do. I had to stay focused on making sure that my son was taken to the hospital so that he could be stabilized and have his medication monitored. The way I did that was to recite my request to God in my mind over and over again. So, while my new friend was watching the officers in my home, I was repeating my request over and over again. Previously, there had been incidences between the police and the Black community that caused the relationship to become strained. As a result, my friend was suspicious because the police were in my home. She wanted me to know what she thought was going on, play by play, and was telling me in my ear. Now, I fully understood where she was coming from and under different circumstances, I would have listened to her and given feedback. In this case, however, that was not happening. I knew that I had to do my part, stay focused, and get out of the way, so God could do His. That was all there was to it.

The interaction between my new friend and I was a great lesson for me. We were two different people, who although had had similar experiences, had very different ideas on how to handle conflict. We, each had strong and valid reasons for seeing things the way we did, and as in these cases, there was no right or wrong answer. This was a gut call—a spirit call or whatever you want to call it. I was relying on something that neither of us could see and she was dealing with what she was seeing. At that point, our communication was ineffective. Neither one of us was being heard or understood. Has that ever happened to you? Have you ever been torn between listening to your friend and listening to God? Are you able to recognize when communication between you and another person becomes ineffective or impossible?

I once heard Iyanla Vanzant say, it is unloving to ask someone to do something that they **cannot** do. I thought about those words in this situation. In this case, I had invited another person into a potentially explosive situation expecting her to support me and I hadn't done my homework. I didn't even check to see if it were possible. Our thoughts, feelings and experiences help to mold us into the persons we become, and help to form what becomes our belief system. She had her story and was entitled to it, just as I was entitled to mine. The unloving part happened when I didn't consider that she may have viewpoints and opinions that were different from my own. And that maybe, she was *unable* to do what I needed her to do. Does that sound familiar?

Has there been a time in your life when you've expected someone to support you or take your side in an issue and they didn't? Have you considered that *their* life experience may limit or prohibit them from supporting yours? In addition to that, when our expectations aren't met, we have nerve to get mad at them!

For me, this was another of those AHA moments and, I realized that this wisdom could apply to other parts of my life. Particularly, during those times when I realize that I am fighting the wrong battle. When I find that I am putting too much time and energy into the wrong things, I have to let it go. In this regard, I knew what had to be done—and I allowed my new friend to leave and I continued in prayer and, oh yes!—God came through.

I learned that you can't forecast how you or anyone else will respond in life changing situations such as this. Therefore, your decisions cannot be based on personality or what somebody else wants you to do or what other people think ought to happen. In the same regard, you don't have the right or the capability to determine what another person can or cannot do. The loving part happens when you can separate the person they are from your own expectations and still be able to care.

## *Miracle #3*

I have been changed. I carry a joy and excitement within me and I look forward to what God has for me each step of the way. When I can help someone else I become a better person. People who know me would probably say that yes, Patrice does try to help people when she can. And you would think that would be enough. But, deep in my heart, I knew there was something missing. And I had to admit to myself I may have been in hiding, so to speak.

It was comfortable for me to connect with people, one-on-one or in small groups and have heart-to-heart talks. However, on the larger stage I stuck to the topics. Topics related to Team Building, Leadership Skills, Assertive Training, Conflict Resolution, Embracing Change and Decision Making, to name a few. My area of expertise allows me to speak on practically any topic that deals with personal and professional development. And that was okay with me, until I started to write this book, or shall I say, allowed it to be written through me.

Now, I love reading and I keep a book with me at all times. I am a book person. Getting to the place where I felt I could sit down and write a book—that's a different story. What scared me most was the idea of being exposed on a larger scale. I was willing to expose myself on a day to day basis, with people I didn't know. But, doing the same thing on a bigger stage caused me to pause. And the funny thing is, I was more concerned with how I would react, than how others might react to me. I thought that somehow I would become someone other than who I am or that I wouldn't like that person. I don't know. But, thinking about it now, I was scared. The truth is, at the time, I didn't know myself.

There is no doubt that my 'mad' and 'ugly' was sitting just below the surface, under the radar, just waiting for the opportunity to take revenge. It happens to all of us. Particularly, when we feel we've been deprived of something or that something was taken away from us. We don't admit or acknowledge these feelings and we allow them to stay hidden—until that one opportunity arises. To the outside world, I always had a smile on my face, yet, on the inside I was held hostage to feelings of doubt, anger and insecurity. And these feelings caused me to be critical and combative, at times.

Once, my son said to me, "you don't act like I'm sick—you aren't supposed to antagonize me". You see, part of his ongoing treatment involves him becoming familiar with his medication, as well as, the symptoms and triggers that cause him to be upset. He knew that when he was struggling with his own emotions, the last thing he needed was to have to deal with mine, unchecked. And instead of keeping it inside and being resentful, he trusted our relationship enough to speak his truth. What that told me was he had learned to look out for himself, and as a result, he was looking out for me as well. What a gift!

And over time, I changed on the inside. I became a listener and an observer in my own life. I was learning that allowing myself to be checked could keep me out of trouble. That meant I had to pay attention to the tightness in my chest, the intense feeling I would get when a 'mad' moment was coming on or the nervous feelings that made me want to run away. And even when that checking came from someone else, I had to be able to hear it. That wasn't always possible in the world, according to Patrice, because, previously, I was the one doing the checking.

## Worth repeating

For you have need or **endurance,** so that after you *have* done the will of God, you may receive the promise: *For yet a little while and He who is coming will come and will not tarry. Now the just shall live, by faith; but if anyone draws back, my soul has no pleasure in him Hebrews10: 36-38*

One of the greatest gifts I have received is the ability to see, first hand, how the word of God has come alive in my life and in the life of others. I am a witness. You know how it is, when you see it for yourself; you realize what *could have happened* and yet, the only word to describe what *did happen* is miracle. It doesn't matter what other people have say about it—you know what it feels like and how it has changed you without a doubt. I know that the words in Hebrew 10:36-38 are true because *I have been a witness.*

The author(s) in Hebrews remind us to 'hang in there' during hardship and to rely on the faith that has brought us to where we are today. During that time in the Bible, people had many questions—and today you have many questions as well. Some of you may wonder why you're still here, or what it is that you could possibly have to offer someone else—after all, you're the one who needs help.

So, rather than debate about what I know versus what you know or get upset if we don't agree—this scripture speaks of benefits and consequences. As a witness, I have experienced the benefits of living by faith and waiting on His promise, while being aware of what the consequences could have been. In that context, I am compelled to continue to let my light shine brightly for all to see, without shame, without excuse.

I have been changed.

## *Food for Thought*

In this section, my desire was to provide some data or statistical information to let you know, that if you or a loved one, is in need of mental health services that 1) you are not alone and 2) there are resources available to you.

However, as I searched for statistical data, I found it to be limited. Statistics are based on reported accounts of utilizing the services available. If we don't use the services we aren't counted. In part, the stigma communities of color associate with mental illness keeps people from seeking the help they need. This in turn impacts the available research and ultimately appropriate treatment.

This is what I have found:

## *U.S. Department of Health & Human Services*

### The Office of Minority Health—Mental Health Data/
### Statistics
### 1-800-444-6472

"Mental health treatment is often underutilized, with patients reluctant to seek these services and insurers reluctant to pay for them. Estimates from a 2001-2003 survey found that about 30% of adults suffered from a mental disorder during the year, yet only one-third of them received treatment . . . From 2005-2006, mental illness was the second most frequent condition, after arthritis, causing activity limitation among adults, ages 18-44 years."

### *Quick Facts*

African Americans are 30% more likely to report having serious psychological distress than Non-Hispanic Whites.

The death rate from suicide for African American men was five times that for African American women, in 2005.

Older Asian American women have the highest suicide rate of all women over age 65 in the United States.

Suicide attempts for Hispanic girls, ages 9-12, were 60% higher than for White girls in the same age group, in 2005.

http://minorityhealth.hhs.gov

Those of you who know there is a problem, you've seen the damage, yet, you are either unwilling or feel unable to get help. There again, you are not alone. That's a common dilemma for us all. We have questions like:

When do I ask for help?
Who do I ask?
What do I do when my loved one is diagnosed?
What if the diagnosis is wrong?
Who can I trust?

Now, it would be wonderful if I could give you the answers, so that you would know what to do, but, that's not how it works.

This is what I know: If you want to find your own answers, you have to ask the right questions. If you want to get to the root of the problem, you have to be willing to be uncomfortable. If you want to find out how you can be of help or get help, you have to go against what other people are saying. If you already know, without having the statistics, that you or your loved one is in danger, you will have to admit that you can't do it alone. If you decide, by any means necessary, that you are in it for the long haul, then you *will need* Jesus.

If you don't know already, the fact that I am upright, alive, healthy and looking forward with anticipation to the rest of my life is because of my relationship with God. It is a relationship founded on the word of God; nurtured by fellowship with His people, saved through the obedience of Jesus Christ, and solidified by faith and belief in the Holy Spirit. It is the only partnership, I have found, that gives me all of the answers that I need.

## *Resources*

**NAMI:** National Association of Mental Illness—A nonprofit, grass roots organization that provides education, support services and advocacy to improve the quality of life of everyone affected by mental illness. Services include an information & referral agency that offers local information about mental illness, classes, support groups, respite care and more.

www.nami.org (800) 950 NAMI (6264)

**National Centers for Mental Health:** www.promoteprevent.org (877) 217-3595

**National Center for Mental Health & Juvenile Justice**

www.ncmhjj.com (866) 9NCMHJJ (626455

**PERT:** Psychiatric Emergency Response Team = Licensed mental health clinicians with uniformed law enforcement officers/deputies who evaluates and assesses the individual's mental health condition and needs.

**PAARTNERS:** Project among African Americans to Explore Risks of Schizophrenia—Psychiatric illnesses such as schizophrenia can cause severe disturbances in a person's mood, belief, and perceptions. They are very common, afflicting over 1% of adults worldwide. African Americans have been understudied and underserved in the mental health area.

PAARTNERS will ensure a comprehensive study of schizophrenia among African Americans. To our knowledge, it is the most

comprehensive study of this kind ever undertaken for any population.
www.soph.uab.edu/paartners/default.htm

| | |
|---|---|
| Crisis/Access Line | (800) 479-3339 |
| Consumer Center for Health | (877) 734-3258 |
| Education & Advocacy | |
| Psychiatric Emergency Response Teams | 911 |
| Adult Abuse Reporting/Crisis Intervention | (800) 510-2020 |
| Social Security Administration | (800) 772-1213 |

## Starting today

When the circumstances in your life seem insurmountable; it may be time for you to stop and develop a new or different strategy for handling hard times; to make the insurmountable, surmountable. Here are 6 strategies that can help:

1. Develop and nurture your relationship with God. Growing up in the church and attending Bible Study gave me a foundation of reading and knowing God's word. As an adult, I wanted to have a personal relationship with God, so I sought out friends who knew the Bible. I attended Bible classes and went to church to hear how God had changed lives in the congregation and preachers alike.

2. Create healthy partnerships. Connect with people you trust. Seek out people with similar situations who have had positive outcomes.

3. Gather information. Contact organizations and service providers who can give you what you need to become knowledgeable and informed.

4. Remember what you already know about yourself and your loved one. Remember, you are the expert. Pay attention to specific changes in behavior and attitude. Use that information to help guide you to the right resources.

5. Get counseling and support for yourself. Ask for referrals—be open and allow God to send the right people your way.

6.  Stay present and in the moment. Sit still and concentrate on your breathing. Take a deep breathe into your diaphragm, hold it for 2 seconds, and slowly blow out the air, through your mouth. Then sit and feel your body relax. Do this 2 to 3 times a day. In those moments, you begin to calm the rat race in your mind. You are present to notice the natural beauty around you. Whether it is the formation of leaves on a tree, the smile on a child's face or the peace that comes from being in the moment. Keep your mind free so that you can make the best decision that it is within your power to make.

And most important of all, **remember that you are not alone!**

# Chapter 3

## Fuel Your Passion, Find Your Own Rhythm

*But we all, with unveiled face, beholding as in a mirror
the glory of the Lord, are being transformed into the same
image from glory to glory, just as by the Spirit of the Lord.*

*2 Corinthians 3:18*

I can say for sure that I have been transformed. You don't go through
the challenges I have faced without being changed or transformed in
some way. The question is, what had I been transformed into?

### Stopped

Well it worked. I poured all of my attention into taking care for my
son and keeping him safe from those who didn't see his genius like
I did. It didn't matter what diagnosis he had been given, he was and
always would be, my son. And I *always* knew that he was a good
person on the inside and that God had our backs. In that regard, I could
say mission accomplished. Having been connected to every resource
available to him, there were many, I was pretty much in charge.

At this point, I was his legal Conservator. Shortly after his diagnosis
(at 16), and before he turned 18 (legal age), one of his doctors
recommended that he be put under conservatorship. I called the
Conservators Office to inquire, had the forms mailed to me and
followed the process. So, I had accumulated a network of Doctors,
Social Workers, Facilities, Pharmacists, State Rehabilitation Agents,

and everything else to ensure that my son was getting the care he needed. So, what now? Well, I'm glad you asked.

During this time, my son was still living with me, and I was once again wearing my **Superwoman** cape. I didn't plan to put it back on—it just happened! You know how we, as women, can get—when we put on our "by any means necessary" attitude—and make the decision to **not** be denied access whatever it takes to complete our mission. Well, in my view, my son's life was my life mission and I was not going to be denied!

Then 3 events happened to change my world, once again.

## *Seeds of faith that I already know what to do —*

The first event happened while I was in Atlanta, at a family wedding. The trip had been planned for some time and my Mom and I were traveling together. I decided that since we were going to be so close, we could hop over to New York to see "The Color Purple", live on Broadway, so I bought the tickets. It would be my first time in New York, as well as, the first time my Mom and I would attend a live production on Broadway. We were very excited.

I mentioned earlier that my son was still living at home with me. That meant I was the one who had to make sure he was taking his medication. The closer I got to the departure date, the more my suspicion grew that he was not taking his medication. Of course, when I asked him about it, he lied and said, "Yeah, I'm taking it" although in my spirit I knew better. To add further stress to the situation, it would be the first time, since his diagnosis, that I would be gone out of town, for a week, without insuring someone was at home with him.

Can you recall one or two, maybe more times when you wanted to make a good decision, however, you didn't see any options that you liked—or wanted to take. Well, I was there. And on top of that, I felt the pressure to find the right answer and to do the right (responsible) thing. In my heart—I was torn.

In this faith walk, I have found that when I try to figure everything out—I am in trouble. And, I know this to be true, yet, time and time again, I suffer from short term memory and fail to remember that I don't have all the answers and I don't have to—for two reasons: 1) If I knew what was going to happen ahead of time—I would do something to mess it up, 2) I already had living proof (case studies in Chapter 5) to confirm that I am here—only by the grace of God. And in this partnership, if you will, I already have a role—and that is, to be the best human being that I can be, on a day to day (minute by minute) basis.

I like to use the expression 'fail to remember' rather than, I forgot, because it lets me know that I need to be either reminded of or need to remember something—and that's okay with me. Those words fall softly into my spirit and I can respond with an "oh yeah" or a "that's right" in the affirmative. Once I am *reminded* of what I already know, and can see myself as God sees me, I can appreciate the joy of **not** having to know it all. It becomes easier to take the next step and to affirm God in our lives.

So, what did I do? I meditated with God, I prayed about it, and got on the plane and went to Atlanta. Oh, by the way, soon after I returned from New York, I had to leave again for a training engagement out of town (I was the trainer).

## Get Over it!

The day before I was to return to San Diego, I got a call from my daughter. She said that something **did** happen at the house, that her brother was safe (sort of) and she had the information for me to follow up when I got home. The fact that she was on top of things helped me to remain calm on my return flight. Although I knew that the incident was directly related to the fact that my son had missed taking his medication, I also knew that I had a direct line to God and that He was always awake anyway. So, I made the call saying "Dear Lord, I need you to keep him safe until I get there" however, it probably sounded more like, Okay Lord, You **gotta** keep him safe . . . **in the name of Jesus!** (Because He already knew how I felt in my heart).

## *Unstoppable*

As I have shared with you, this was not the first time my son had stopped taking his medication. Not even the first five to ten times (actually I lost count) and just like many of you, I had made promises to God to get myself out of trouble before, so I was familiar with the process. Whether it was, *Lord, if you just help me this time, I'll never do it again* or *I'll do the right thing NEXT time*! My son liked to point out the things that I've said I would do and didn't follow through on—to call me out, if you will—so I made the connection, while also recognizing the full gravity of this situation. And I didn't take it personally, nor was I angry when my son lied to me about taking his medication. I had laid out the consequences several times; that if he didn't take it, he couldn't live with me. And my son had stopped taking his medication (once again). So, the ball was clearly in my court.

One of the hardest things I've had to do is to follow through with consequences when I didn't want to, even though I knew I had to. Pause for an **Amen!**

Whether I *really believed* my son's diagnosis or not, I had seen (lot of times) what would happen when he had stopped taking his medication. And, therefore I knew I already had the answer. So what was my problem? Part of me was confused in my new role. I had spent so much time being in control of everything, that I wasn't sure what my new role would look like. I had questions like:

> Aren't I *supposed* to put my life on hold for my son?
> Would it really help if I did?
> If I put him out, where would he live?
> How can I control things if he lives somewhere else?
> How can I live a full "normal" life if he can't?
> Am I worthy enough to deserve my own life?

Most importantly, would my son still love me if I didn't let him come home? Is home really where the heart is? The thing that pulled at my heart strings the most was that he always wanted to come home. My son is a home body and the guilt of not allowing him to do the one thing that he wanted to do, tore me up inside.

I didn't have any answers to those questions. As you can see, all of my questions were related to what might happen in the future. It would have been much easier if I knew what would happen next. But, in reality, all I had was what I was given to do in this moment. Isn't that something—once again I was **reminded** that I already had the answer to what I needed to do. And I already had a strategy that I knew worked.

So, I asked myself the 3 questions (my formula) that help me to focus:

1.  Is my *intention* to help my son?
2.  Have I *made up my mind* to keep him and those around him safe?
3.  Is *God's grace* still alive and well?

If the answer was YES to all three questions, and there weren't extenuating circumstances, then I have to move forward and do what I said I would do. And, so I did. By this time, I was no longer using consequences as a control mechanism or a threat designed to change his behavior. My decision was based on the fact that I could not keep my son safe and keep him at home, at the same time.

Another part of my formula is to tell my son the truth in the moment. This did not come naturally to me, I had to learn it. This piece of wisdom was given to me by a beloved Pastor's wife, Dr. Louilyn Hargett. This particular Sunday, I was feeling quite frustrated, overwhelmed and a little bit defeated. I needed help with my teenager (who happened to have a mental illness). You see, there were times when I didn't know if I was talking to the teenager in him, or the illness in him, or both. So, I asked Dr. Louilyn what she did when her children were teenagers. And she said, "Tell them the truth—I just tell them the truth". I remember she said it with such confidence and in such a matter of fact way that I believed her.

To be able to tell the truth of what is happening, in the moment, without emotion, blame or critical analysis was a new concept to me. I always believed in being honest, however, I realized that in trying to protect my children, I had become a little preachy . . . I was talking at them and not to them . . . I would argue down a point until they admitted I was right, because after all, **I was!**

So, since that day I had become better at talking and listening to my son. When we discussed a specific event or situation, I learned to stay focused on events as they happened and not get distracted by trying to make a point. I don't know about the children you know, but my son is a genius at leading me down the path he wants me to take, and getting me totally off topic. A conversation might go like this:

**Mom:** Son, I've told you several times before that in order to live with me, you have to take your medication.

**Son**: No you didn't! And why am I taking medication anyway! There's nothing wrong with me, you're the one who keeps putting me in the hospital. There's nothing wrong with me! You're probably the one who is sick! You need to be on medication! When I get older I'm going to put YOU in the hospital . . . !!!!

And after much practice, I learned to lovingly respond.

**Mom:** Son, I've told you several times before that in order to live with me you have to take your medication. And I know that you haven't been taking it because you aren't eating or taking care of yourself like you usually do. You been sleeping, off and on, for the last two days *and* I found some of your pills on the floor in your bedroom.

You see, I don't believe that a child owns a bedroom until they can actually buy a house and since my name was on the deed to this one, I owned his bedroom. There is a difference between getting the information you need to support your family and crossing some invisible line into what they call disrespect. I had already established a baseline to distinguish between the two. I remember what a friend of mine in Law Enforcement once said to me, "Patrice, I go into kids bedrooms and the whole room is green (in a gang color), and the parent's don't even notice or say anything".

So, I learned to do my homework before opening my mouth. I knew what was considered his 'normal' behavior—I had studied him and had taken notes. I mean literally—I have file drawers, boxes and notebooks filled with my notes, documentation and forms. Therefore, I knew what I was talking about. If anyone was able to speak in truth, it was me. I was confident in that. I'd also informed him that I was committed to do whatever I had to do and to go wherever I had to go to give him the support he needed and to keep him, and myself safe.

When I did the best I could do; if I was wrong I would apologize. I understood that we were both fighting for the same thing—for his life—we just had different perspectives on to *how* to go about it.

Upon my return from New York (I had pre-arranged with his Doctor to have him hospitalized to get his medications back in track), I told him the truth. That I was taking him to the hospital and I wanted him to cooperate with me and that I had to leave town again for a training gig. And that is exactly what happened—I checked him into the hospital, went back home to pack and left for my training engagement soon after. When I returned home I let him know that he could no longer live with me. It's all about timing.

## Seeds of letting go and trusting God

## Stopped

The second thing that happened served to push me further out of my protective comfort zone. As a full time employee/retiree, I had full coverage private insurance provided by my employer. That gave me the confidence to know that my family had access to what I felt was the best hospitals, doctors and facilities available. After it was clear to me that my son could no longer live with me, I knew that initially, he would have to go into a facility that provided 24 hour care and support. Now he had been to various facilities before, but this time, I was informed that I had to drop him from *my* (comfy, protective) insurance coverage and allow the County to take over all of his medical/mental health needs. Of course, I knew this day would come—but at a later date. Technically, I had another year before he had to be dropped. NOT RIGHT NOW!

I wasn't ready. But, as often happens in my life, I found out—it wasn't about me!

## Unstoppable

I don't know how I was able to make the call. Maybe I was tired, or my brain had temporarily shut down or it may have been I had no choice. In my mind, having private insurance was my leverage—it gave me the ability to call the shots or appear to anyway. And now I was being told I had to give it up. As I reached for the phone, I remember a sense of calm came over me. In that moment I was able to cancel the medical insurance that I had provided for my son since the day he was born.

Life for me felt pretty hectic as my children were growing up. It seemed to be full of frantic movement, anxiety and constant bargaining to give them the best I had to offer. Much like you, regardless of our level of ability to provide the best—as parents, guardians, caregivers, grandparents, etc.—we want to.

And now, in spite of what I wanted to do—as if in a trance—I had to do what I was told to do, regardless of how I felt about it. After that I sat back and waited for the other shoe to fall. I'm not sure what I thought would happen, but, I can tell you truthfully, that nothing did. From that day forward the quality and level of services that my son receives has not changed or wavered.

This was another lesson in trust—no matter how old our children get, they are always precious in our eyes. I was slowly learning to put the lives of those most precious to me, totally in God hands; trusting that, in spite of what happens or how it looks on the outside, everything would work out!

*Seeds—turning it all over to God*

*Stopped*

The third thing that happened was about me. It was all about me. Everything had been piling up . . . my superwoman cape was really wearing thin, my nerves were frazzled and staff from the facility, where my son stayed, were calling frequently. My son was being uncooperative and disruptive and nothing the staff did made a difference. They had scheduled a meeting and since I was his conservator, and had been for the past 8 1/2 years, I had to attend.

Again it's all about timing.

This was all part of the process—I was used to being called in to get through to my son when no one else could. I would charge in with my 'bottom line' attitude, setting boundaries and negotiating, to get my son to agree to a plan designed to improve his life. However, this time, I was done!! I had run out of ideas and I felt as if my brain had shut down. I was beyond being *tired*, and the last thing I wanted to do was to attend another meeting. In fact, I had given myself a time-out and was spending a few nights at my cousin's home. I had privacy and quiet during the day while she was working, and her company in the evening when she came home. And she liked to cook. So, it was all good—until I got that call.

On this same day, another cousin of ours just happened to call the house (imagine that!) and when I saw her number, I answered the phone. As I was giving her a summary of why I was there, I told her about the call I had just gotten summoning me to the dreaded meeting. She listened to me and then, in another moment of grace, she asked me if I wanted her to go to the meeting with me. Now, prior to this day, I had never thought about asking or *allowing* anyone to go to a meeting with me—1) I didn't need any help 2) Although my mother and daughter had visited my son when he was hospitalized—I wasn't sure if anyone else could handle entering a locked psychiatric facility when they didn't have to. So, even though I was surprised when she asked the question, I was also done! I was tired. I needed help. So, I said yes. I even let her drive me to the meeting.

As my cousin and I sat on one side of the table, the staff members and treatment coordinator working with my son sat on the other. He was not in the room yet. They wanted to talk to me first to let me know what had prompted this meeting, and to tell me that if my son's behavior didn't change, he would be evicted from the facility. They explained that if he were evicted, as his conservator, **I** would be responsible for finding housing for him or taking him home with me. While my mind was stuck (or in shock) on that last thought, my son entered the room.

I could tell by the way he entered the room that we were in trouble. Everything from the clothes he chose to wear; to the way he wore them; to the way he slid into the chair told us loud and clear I AM NOT COOPERATING TODAY! As I said earlier, even when the staff couldn't get through to him, I always could. But, that was not happening—he had shut me out too. So, after a few minutes, he got up and left the room.

## *Get over it!*

As I was trying to digest what would happen if he were evicted, an *angel spoke* through the voice of the Treatment Coordinator who had called the meeting. She said, *maybe it's time for you to stop being his conservator.* Although I had been doing this for a long time, I hadn't thought about turning it over to someone else. It was as if a window had been opened for me. I felt drained of emotion, yet, at the same time I knew I was being set free. I was getting an opportunity to regain my strength, to regroup and to be available to my son in a way that I had never been able to before. It was time—I was ready and I knew it would be alright.

## *Unstoppable*

I call it a glimpse of clarity. It is the place where you see all that it has taken to get where you are, in that moment in time in that snapshot you recognize that if you keep doing what you've always done, **you** may not make it. Was it my objective to see how much I could take before I needed to be hospitalized myself, or did I want to be healthy and think clearly so that I could fully support and oversee my son's treatment and care? Was God trying to tell me something?

Earlier in this chapter, I shared thoughts that caused me to question myself and the motivation behind my actions. I believe they are worth repeating—for those who may have the same thoughts, it may help.

> Aren't I *supposed* to put my life on hold for my son?
> Would it really help if I did?
> If I put him out, where would he live?
> How can I control things if he lives somewhere else?
> How can I live a full "normal" life if he can't?
> Am I worthy enough to deserve my own life?

Most importantly, would my son still love me if I don't let him come home? Because as I said before, having to tell my son that he couldn't come home again, left a hole in my heart that I wasn't sure would be filled.

And after that, is there a life just for me? I was torn once again because I had heard all of my life that it was not good to be *selfish*. So, I went to my friend, Mr. Webster's dictionary and found something very interesting. I looked up the words, self-interest, selfish and selfless and the definitions are as follows: self-interest = one's own interest or advantage, an exaggerated regard for this; selfish = overly concerned with one's own interest and having little concern for others; selfless = devoted to others' welfare, unselfish. It appeared to me, by using words such as: advantage, exaggerated regard, overly-concerned, little concern for and devoted to others' welfare, that I may not be the only one bothered by the word *selfish*.

The main problem I had is that people were using the word like a weapon. If someone felt you cared too much for yourself or had your own personal desires, they would whip it out and cut you down with it. Can you hear it? Has someone said to you, "YOU ARE SOOOOO SELFISH!!!?

As if there wasn't room for balance between being selfish and taking care for yourself—and for me, balance is right up there with *timing,* as far as importance in my life.

So, I chose these words as the model for my life. *Self—care.* It acknowledges that our *self* (each one of us) is the greatest gift God has given to us. *So God created man in His own image; in the image of God He created him; male and female He created them.* Geneses 1:27. And my responsibility, I believe, is to take care of what God has created in His image—me.

Then, in order to run the race that God has set for me, while taking better care of those entrusted to me, I have to create balance in my life. Balance for me, means taking *care* of myself first. That way I can easily get in touch with my own joy, instead of letting you see my ugly side. Which shows up when I have given so much of me away that I feel deprived and abandoned (mad about Dad) once again. And you can be a witness to the fact that in order to be my best and give my best, I have to take care of the gift—that is me.

## Self—Care

I understand how past experiences can cause us to feel 'less than' or 'not enough' and therefore, we can be our own worst critic.

> **Dispel the lies:** When I have negative thoughts that seem to come out of nowhere, I pause and ask myself—Where did that come from? In other words, I question whether those thoughts are true about me and my intention, or is it a lie.

> **Stay connected to my truth:** Once I have determined what is true about me, I stick to it! One day I was taking my son to

school and he was upset with me. So, he proceeded to tell me all the ways that I was intentionally messing up his life. In the past, I would have felt the need to defend myself, however, this time I didn't respond. As I drove home, after dropping him off, I thought "that is not me. It was not my intention, nor has it ever been, to mess up his life". That was my truth.

**I am enough just as I am:** After spending too much time thinking about how different my life would be, if only . . . I realized that this is the only life that I know about. It is my gift from God. And as such, I needed to appreciate and honor who I am, rather than put myself down.

## Getting the message

I was listening to a sermon by my Pastor, Rev. Reginald L. Gary and he was using Mark 2:1-12 as the basis for his message. It didn't matter to me that he was directing the majority of his sermon to the men of the church (it was close to Father's Day), I have learned that if I am in the room, then the message is for me. So, as he spoke about encouragement and commitment, he said that we all have a destiny and a divinely planned purpose for our lives. As I listened to those words, I thought, yes! God has a plan just for me! Reverend Gary went on to say, **things may change within the mission, but the mission never changes.** It was as if he were speaking directly into my heart. And in my heart, I was ready to receive the message.

## Food for thought

Was part of my dilemma based on disbelief? That old thinking that if I don't do it, who will! That *somebody* had to be a sacrifice for my son. I was raised in the church and I had read the New Testament many, many times and I *knew* the story. The book of Matthew, the apostle and former tax collector, provides a detailed look into the birth, life, death and resurrection of Jesus Christ. I have spoken about it, sang about it and prayerfully thanked God for sending His son, Jesus as a sacrifice for the sins of man. That being said, why on earth was I still thinking that *somebody else* had to be the sacrifice for my son, when I *knew* it had already been taken care of?

I think my ego had slipped in when I wasn't looking, and instead of thanking God for the sacrifice, I was suffering from a condition that caused me to edge God out. Have you ever had that condition where you actually believed that **you** had the power to save somebody else, or save yourself, for that matter? I mean deep down on the inside. After all, if we had that kind of power, we could use it to stop worrying and actually eliminate the fear of what might happen next. The truth is, for some of us, worry and fear have become a full-time job.

Getting to a place where through it all and no matter how it looks, we can trust God totally is like having an out of this world experience. Since we can't *see how* God's miracles work, we have to believe in something that is beyond our physical world. And that is usually preceded by our request for God to bring us safely through a situation that is so devastating we wouldn't wish it on anyone else. The reason we call it a 'spiritual walk' is because we don't walk it with other people, we walk it with Jesus Christ. Now God does send people into your life to walk with you and help you along the way. However, I can tell you from experience, that you need to check to **make sure** that it was **God** who sent them.

I mentioned earlier that having a partnership with God is twofold. It means that 1) I learn my part and 2) I do what I have learned to do. Then I can always count on God to do His part. I have found I am better able to do my part and to hear God's message when my head and heart are working in unison.

The truth is that we are an intellectual people. We are thinkers, and are sometime prone to believe that knowledge alone, head stuff, is all we need. Yes, our minds can hold a lot of information, however, working alone, may not give us the filters we need to make the right decision. We carry around thoughts about ourselves and other people that would make you cringe, if we said it out loud. Most of these thoughts are outdated, have never been verified, have no corroborating data to support them or are downright lies. And we carry this stuff around!

When we want to get deeply into the emotion of a situation, we say that we are getting to the heart of the matter. The heart is usually the core of where our emotions lie, and allows us to connect to one another in sympathy, sadness, joy or love. Sometime the heart is said to be the soft spot in each of us. To trust the heart solely, without boundaries, could get us into trouble. In short, the heart can be reached by the right touch or a notion that, if you REALLY love me . . . you will do what I want you to do . . . **Pause for prayer.**

In order to train the head and heart to work together, we will have to fill our minds with good things. *Finally Brethren, whatever things are true, whatever things are noble, whatever things are just, whatever things are pure, whatever things are lovely, whatever things are of **good report,** if there be any virtue and if there is anything praiseworthy—meditate on these things.* Philippians 4:8.

And place these words in our hearts. *But above all these things put on love, which is the bond of perfection. And let the **peace of God rule in your hearts**, to which also you were called in one body, and be thankful.* Colossians 3:14-15. Getting to this place in head and heart takes time and your full attention, as well as, the belief that you deserve the best.

## Starting today

My passion hadn't changed. I've always wanted to help people and make a difference in the world. I've wanted to help women in particular to move beyond their circumstances and choose the life they both desire and deserve to have. I knew it was possible. I just wasn't sure how I was *supposed* to do it. I didn't want to get it wrong.

What I have learned is that when you are true to your God given, divinely planned purpose, and continually ask Him for guidance, you can't get it wrong.

## *Do you like you?*

In chapter 1, I asked you to create a list of things you like about yourself; to serve as a reminder that you are already likeable, just as you are. My hope is that when you connect to what is good in you; that you will begin to see the value and brilliance you bring to the world. The goal being, when you acknowledge to yourself that you're not a burden and that you actually like yourself, that you will treat yourself as you would a good friend. Remember, you are not the enemy.

Take some time and think about a previous or a current situation where you have done all that you can think to do; have used up every emotion in your being; cried until your ducts are dry, and still, nothing has changed. Check in and notice how your body is responding in those moments. Does your heart rate speed up? Are you feeling anxious and panicky? Does your head feel fuzzy? In that state, if an emergency arose, would you be able to think clearly enough to help someone else, or even help yourself?

Now, wait for several minutes—take slow deep breaths and allow your body to become calm. Think of a situation where you were relaxed and having a good time. It could be when you and a friend were talking and laughing together, or you spent time with a loved one or you were thinking about how blessed you are as a family. Go to that place. Now, check in with your body. Do you feel relaxed? Have things inside of you slowed down enabling you to be in the moment? Has your great sense of humor and quick wit reappeared? In this state, could you think clearly and quickly in an emergency?

Just a shift in the way you think about yourself can give you balance in your life. It could mean the difference between life or sudden death; between making a living or making a life and can enable you to hear God's mission for your life or not.

## *Your steps have been ordered*

Look back at your life and think about the path that has brought you to where you are today. Can you follow the steps and see how each one has brought you to this place in your life? And that if you are still here, it's a good day—because that means there is more for you to do. When things went well for you and worked out, what was the formula?

Ask yourself: What was your part in it? In your best moments, what did you do that made a positive difference? Is it a strategy that you can apply in other areas of your life? You see, in partnership with God, it is our best that He wants from us.

Make a list, study on those things that bring out the best in you, so that you can recognize the best in others. Learn and study your part so that your mind and heart can be free to *hear* what God wants you to do.

## *Open to Divine Guidance*

This is how I do it:

Earlier, I gave you my formula for being present and staying in the moment. It is to "dispel the lies, to stay connected to my truth and to remember that I am enough just as I am". I was able to get to that point because I have learned how to quiet my life. We have many things that keep us from finding time to be still and just be. What I have found is that when I take 5 minutes, before I start my day, to sit quietly, take a few deep breaths and relax, I actually get more done. And, I feel better about it. When I find myself rushing around frantically, I remember what I can do to make myself feel better, without drugs. I take moments to focus on my body and my breathing throughout the day.

Also, I allow myself to periodically check out of what is going on in society. I tune out the noise of all the stuff other people think I ought to be doing or the latest technology I need to have and spend time with God. I still communicate with loved ones and take care of those things that need to be done—I just get out of the mainstream. I quiet my world so that I can listen and learn. I meditate on my life and scripture and I get reinforcement from spiritual partners on things that I need to discuss. I don't judge anything or anyone, not even myself. I started doing this for 1 or 2 hours at a time, and then, as time permits, I stay in the process longer. Doing this lets me get to my internal place of peace and be open to hear what God has for me.

When I have a difficult decision to make, my best strategy is to do my homework—and gather pertinent information—ask for input from those I respect, remember who I am and then let it percolate overnight. In other words, I turn it over to God and I sleep on it. Usually I am awakened about 3 or 4 in the morning, and I have the answer.

This practice is effective for me because I have found it works. The key to you finding your best strategy is solely based on what you have discovered works for you.

# Chapter 4

## Be Present, Live on Purpose—Walk Your Talk

*To everything there is a season, A time*
*for every purpose under Heaven:*
*A time to love, and A time to hate; A time of war,*
*and A time of peace.*

*Ecclesiastes 3:1, 8*

We've all had personal experiences in life that serve to smack us upside our heads or to touch our hearts in a way that changes us forever. It may involve the loss of a job, or divorce that breaks the family apart or the loss of a loved one. If we lose someone young, we tend to say *gone to soon.* If our loved one is older we tend to focus on how honored we were to have been a part of their life.

When my Aunt Wilma left us at the age of 101—I was so honored to have been with her as we celebrated her 100th birthday, a little more than a year before. At 100 years old, she had the same energetic, witty, spirited, life-loving and caring spirit that she had all of her life. She knew, without a doubt, that God had always taken care of her; that her children loved her and they loved to spend time with her. My Aunt Wilma was excited about each new day. She told me that herself. Through her life I have seen the amazing Grace of God and how seeds planted by her parents had sprouted in the way she loved and cared for her husband and her children. Her life reflected her unyielding faith in God.

The truth is, no matter what we think or believe, we are never ready for someone we love to leave us.

## *Stopped—my daughter*

I had 3 children—2 daughters and a son. My second child, Vivian (VC) didn't get the chance to grow up as my other children did. As she was being delivered the doctor told me that the umbilical cord was wrapped around her neck. I don't remember how long it took, but, they finally got the cord from around her neck. I was told she had lost oxygen during the delivery. However, when she was checked out and released to go home, I didn't think any more about it.

The one thing I remember is that VC cried more than my first child. Other than that, there wasn't anything different.

A few months after she was born, I was in the bedroom checking on her. She had been asleep in her crib. I could see from the door that she was moving around, even though she was quiet. And, as I reached into the crib to pick her up, I noticed that her body was making a jerking motion. She seemed to be having a convulsion. What happened next is still a blur.

When we got to the hospital, we were told that her body temperature has risen so quickly that it sent her into convulsions. Even then, I didn't make any connection to the *loss of oxygen* during her delivery. I heard the words *possible brain damage* and *Cerebral Palsy*, but, I had no idea what that meant in terms of the impact on her young life. The doctors stabilized her condition, gave us a prescription for anti-convulsion medication, and we took her home.

After taking VC to the Pediatrician for her regular check-up, I realized that nothing had changed in her development. She was not alert or responding to stimulation in a way that was expected from a growing baby. No matter what they said or didn't say—the truth is the doctor's had the same questions that I had—and no one had the answers. As her mom, I felt guilty.

After all, I was the one who carried her for nine months—was it something I did or didn't do to cause this to happen? How did the umbilical cord get around her neck in the first place? I didn't *feel* any differently carrying her, although I had gained a little more weight. So, I didn't know what to think.

I was young. At this point in my life I didn't recognize that my grandparents had planted seeds for our family to have favor for generations to come. Nor was I spiritually mature enough to acknowledge God's grace in my life. My viewpoint of being in a relationship with God was based on the assumption that, because I was human, I had to be guilty of something. And, as a result, I felt helpless and guilty—for a little while.

I don't know when my feelings of guilt and helplessness changed into determination to get the help we needed. I just know that something changed inside of me. It may have been the fact that there were no answers to my questions, and after a while, I felt like I was going in circles—I'm not sure. What I do know is that within each of us is a level of resolve that allows us to stand in our truth when we need to and to not be moved. Eventually, I understood it to be the voices of my grandparents telling me that, "when we encountered tough times, as we often did, we didn't complain—we just went to work".

So, I moved forward in search of resources and options to help me determine what to do next.

I know that my life has been touched by circumstances that can either cause me to falter in my faith or to strengthen it beyond a shadow of a doubt. I understand this to be part of the deal that comes with being human. But, just because I know it's the deal doesn't make it any easier; for me or for you.

In my search to find the right resources to help VC to get better—two things became clear. I would not find the resources to reverse or to change her condition, and I could not keep her at home and provide the care that she needed. As a result, she spent a lot of her life being cared for by other people . . . All I could do was to make sure that she got the medical care that she needed.

## Stopped again

It was a Saturday. I was at work. I got the call from the doctor that VC had passed on. He said that she died in her sleep. VC was ten years old and even though she didn't get to do any of the things that other children are able to do; she greatly impacted the hearts of those of us who love her and continue to miss her.

## Unstoppable Seeds

Initially, I hadn't thought to put this part of my life in the book. However, when I sent the draft to my daughter, an Ordained Minister, she reminded me that it needed to be included. And as I have often found, when my children become my teachers, I need to listen.

Having to go back in my mind and sit in those moments has shifted me once again. I knew I had done all that I could. But, I didn't acknowledge my feelings of guilt out loud, so to speak, and I found that some still lingered deep in my soul.

Now, being removed from that young woman of my youth and my thinking at that time, I can see things more clearly. Whether I get the answers to my questions or not, I accept what is and trust that God is in total control. And, the longer I live, the more I understand that my life has a divine purpose. As such, I have to release, within myself, those emotions that serve to keep me stuck.

## Stopped—my brother

I was returning from a conference in Long Beach when my cell phone rang. It was my niece, and she was saying something about my brother. I remember hearing the words that her Uncle Eric, my brother, had died and I heard the pain in her voice, but I couldn't respond to it. Remember, I am the oldest child, so I immediately thought about my Mom. After all, this was her only son and her youngest child.

My friends dropped me off to pick up my car and I went straight to my Mom's house. From that moment on, I went into action. When I walked into my Mother's living room, I could see the anguish, shock and disbelief in her face, so I thought it best to get to work. There was so much to do. We had to come together as a family, (as you know that ain't always easy) and decide how we would travel to San Luis Obispo (where my brother lived). Once we got there we had to figure out what we were going to do—all in one week.

Well, we made it! My Mom decided to have the service in San Luis Obispo where my brother had established his new life. The celebration of his life was intimate, personal and full of laughter. My daughter presided over the service and we all took part as we remembered those things we cherished about my brother. As it turned out, my nephew and cousin-in-law had us laughing out loud as they recalled similar stories about him. His friends shared funny stories as they talked about how much he meant to them. He loved it there and his friends loved him.

The amazing thing to us is how well he lived in his new life. Now, I like the say that God has a sense of humor because he put my brother, as the youngest child, in a family with three older sisters. Our Dad died when he was 13 months old and so basically, he was in trouble. We didn't know what to do with him and he didn't know what to do about us. Oftentimes, he was just there—kind of in the way. Don't get me wrong, we loved him, we just didn't understand him. Although we stayed in contact, he had moved out of San Diego more than 10 years ago, so we didn't really know *how* he was living. Through our Mom, we knew that he was becoming more and more independent and making good life decisions, however, we didn't know what that looked like.

Those of us who could make the trip had traveled to San Luis Obispo—including his daughters—Sarah and Vanessa, grandsons he hadn't met—Chase and Terrell and Sarah's husband, Terrell

Jr. We entered my brother's home and found that he had not only established a new life, he had created a home that reflected all that we'd hoped for him. He had found his place of peace. In his home, there was a place for everything and everything had its place.

The only picture in sight was one of his daughters, and that meant the world to them. My brother wasn't always expressive with his love and, so for them, this was confirmation that he kept them in his thoughts and heart.

My brother's home was decorated to reflect both his eclectic taste and his adventurous spirit—he had knee high wading boots and all the fishing gear to go with it; a guitar, three keyboards, several other instruments, very nice furniture, a great music sound system with a vast collection of videos and music from the old-school sounds to the latest, as well as, his 52" wide screen television. He also collected commemorative coins. It was evident that he had an eye for value in the items he purchased and he took care of them. In fact, I noticed that he had very good taste. Who would've thought . . . we just didn't know. We were still thinking about the baby brother that we knew from when he was little and kind of messy. Not only had my brother turned his life around; he was living a life that any mother, my mother was proud of. And that was enough for me.

It was heartwarming to hear the outpouring of love from those who knew him in this new place—we already knew that he was happy there. After the service, my sister was driving us through the town of San Luis Obispo—we were leaving. As I sat in the back seat I reflected on the time my brother had picked me up from the airport (I was conducting a training in the area) and took me on a tour of the downtown area.

He knew all the landmarks and the best places to eat. I also got a glimpse of how it felt to live there, because he also knew the attitudes of the people and I could see how his life had become interwoven with theirs. He appreciated what he had and he took care of it, including how he behaved as a good citizen and a contributor in his community. Before returning to the airport he took me to meet a man who was a mentor to him—who helped him to keep his life focused and moving forward. In that moment, I knew he would be okay.

As I was caught up in my memories, I realized that this would be the last time I'd be in this area in connection with my brother. The impact of that thought hit me like a wave that starts slowly and then builds to tremendous heights. Tears slowly began to roll down my face and then, in an instant an avalanche of emotions erupted inside of me. Before I knew it, my face had twisted up and my mouth was open and my body trembled uncontrollably in the disbelief of grief. The impact of that phone call from my niece has finally hit me. And it was safe to let go. My brother was gone—he was 51 years young—he had found his place of peace—and I could no longer see or speak to him in this physical world. Now, I had to keep him close in my heart.

## *Get Over it!*

I knew something inside of me had changed. A sense of urgency had entered my life. Not in the way of frantically running around with my hands in the air yelling "the sky is falling", but in a way that took me back to my quiet place. A place where I knew I had a divine purpose and it was time for me to get off my butt and get on with it.

I believe that I have always walked my talk, at least I've tried to, but, I didn't always follow through. Do you remember those '*come to Jesus"* moments in your my life when you promise to go all the way—to step into your brilliance—to be all that God wants you to be? Well, I do—*more than once*. Shortly after making that plea I suddenly became aware of my short comings; my feelings of insecurity would rise up and take hold of me and I would become like Moses in Exodus 4, who said to Jesus, *O my Lord, I am not eloquent, neither before nor since You have spoken to Your servant; but I am slow of speech and slow of tongue*. Regardless of how powerful others tell you that you are or what you know about your gifts and talents, it is a different thing entirely when you have been called out by God—to get over it, get off your butt and to get busy.

## Unstoppable

I have felt the pain of loss in friendships before. My best girlfriends (my buds), in Junior High School, were Diana, Linda and Phyllis. We would walk home from school together and had maintained our friendship over the years, even though life had taken us in different directions. That was my original crew, my "girls". Sadly, today, I am the only one who is still here. Truth be told, I can still hear their voices and I do *talk to them* from time to time, even though they can no longer talk to me. I am still honored to have been a part of their lives and yes, they were gone too soon. I still feel privileged to have been in their lives and to have shared many precious moments together.

However, when my brother died, something inside of me had changed—my perspective had shifted, once again. I was able to see how privileged I was in other areas of my life.

## About Richard Pryor

For instance, one of the things I had gotten from my brother was the Richard Pryor Live on the Sunset Strip video. In the video, Richard talks about his previous relationships, his marriage; his challenge with drugs; the accident that caused his burn injuries and the visit from his friend, Jim Brown. As I watched the video, I realized what an honor it is to have 'grown up' with Richard Pryor, where I could witness his pure genius, first hand. Whether I had seen him in person or not, I felt like I knew him. I felt like I had a front row seat into his life. I got a sneak peek into his friendship with Jim Brown and others like myself who loved him, regardless of his flaws.

In a part of the video, Richard talks about how he had been in his room for weeks, smoking crack and that finally, his "ole lady called Jim Brown" to come over and check on him. When Jim came in, he didn't bring judgment, or reproof or disgust at seeing his friend smoke crack in front of him, he just had one question. He asked Richard, watcha gonna do? It was comical watching Richard tell about how Jim followed him around his house asking the same question over and over again. No matter what Richard did or said, Jim stayed focused on the question, watcha gonna do? I could see how that visit made an impression on Richard, because as a viewer it had an impact on me. During times of struggle and uncertainty in my life, I hear this voice in my head asking, watcha gonna do (and I smile) as if those words were meant just for me.

## About Oprah Winfrey

I also recognize the privilege in living with Oprah Winfrey. Not literally, of course. She has touched my life in ways too numerous to count. Remember the story of my ancestors in Arkansas in the 1900's—they could not have imagined that their children, in our lifetime, would be honored to see God's grace in such a person as Oprah. Rather than try to explain the impact she has had on my life; I will say that the reason that I am able to write this book and embrace the full meaning behind it is because of Oprah. She showed me what life can look like, when you allow it to be used for a greater purpose. And with that, she gave me a blueprint for handling success with grace and humility.

The idea of using my life to help other people was always in the back of my mind. But, the thought of my life being bigger than I had imagined scared me. Maybe I thought I would get out of control or do something so wrong I'd mess up my blessing (here we go—that I would get it wrong?) so it was easier not to do anything. However, you can't hide from yourself (that's a song). And it is through Oprah's life and the ease in which she lives it (comfortably in her own skin) that has allowed me to see, once again, that God is still in charge.

I can trust that He will keep me in check as long as I stay focused on my mission—and allow my own life to be used in a way that I had not imagined before. Oprah showed up and allowed the world to walk with her, step by step, through her life; to grow with her; to cry with her and to just be who we are with her. And the coolest thing is she is showing us, once again, that re-inventing our lives can look pretty good.

## About Maya Angelou

Also courtesy of Oprah, through her newest venture, OWN network, I watched a Master Class featuring, whom I consider to be one of God's greatest gifts to us, Maya Angelou. I too, grew up reading her books, the first being "I Know Why The Caged Birds Sing", and listening to her poetry as he weaves her words of wisdom into everything she does. On the show, I watched her at 82 years young talk about how fabulous her 60's were, and how much better the 70's were to her and now that she is in her 80's, she advises us to get there if we can. And then, she sang an African American song from the 19th Century (my grandparents might have sang it also), *"when it look like the sun wouldn't shine anymore, God put a rainbow in the clouds"*. That was it, just those two lines and before I knew it, I was having a *hallelujah* time, right in my living room. I played back it several times.

Then this great, wise, gracious voice said, that when she has to speak, she brings everybody who has ever been kind to her—from all races, background and beliefs—to the stage with her and that she never feels like she doesn't have help. And in her most humble way, she called us to prepare ourselves to be a rainbow in somebody else's cloud—to be a blessing to somebody else. What a blessing she is to us all. ***Pause to absorb***. I believe that great messages and great words deserve our full attention. It is important for me to take a moment, to be still and let those words sit in my soul; to resonate inside of me, so that I don't miss the gift.

## About my Mom

I am also honored to be the daughter of Mable Diggs Henderson. You see, all of the things that I see in others as mentioned above, I also see in my mother. Like Richard Pryor, my mother has jokes—she is a funny lady with a great sense of humor. Like Jim Brown, she asks the all-important, life altering question, Pat, *what* were you thinking?

Like Oprah, she showed up. When my dad died, in that instant her life was thrust onto a bigger stage, one that she had not seen coming. Yet, she didn't complain about it, or fight it or run away from it. My mom was a young widow with four children and she kept it moving. She took center stage and walked her family into the right places, with the right people whom she felt carried the same values and beliefs as those she grew up with (the seeds).

It is a privilege for me to witness when people (young and old) approach my Mom and tell her how she has been a positive influence in their lives. Whether it was when she worked for San Diego City Schools, through the church, her Sorority or out in the community. Some of their comments have been, "you pushed me to do better, because of you I have achieved . . . ." Her friends say, that if you want something done, give it to my Mother. I have nicknamed her the ever-ready bunny rabbit because she just keeps going, and going, and going . . . And like Maya Angelou, she continues to be a rainbow in many people's clouds, including mine.

## Food for thought

Reflect on the people in your life, who have had the greatest influence on who you are today, whether they are still here or not. Ask yourself, as a result of knowing this person, how have I grown? What have I learned as a result of hearing their inspiring stories or reading about their lives? How am I different because of the people who have the courage to tell me the truth, whether I wanted to hear it or not. What about those people who have loved you and taken care of you, in spite of the obstacles they had to face? Think about the people who have stuck with you, and are still standing beside you; those who do so because they've made a commitment and to do otherwise was not acceptable. Those people who have been your rainbow on a cloudy day. Have you told them or showed them in some way what they really mean to you?

## Starting today

Seek out the people in your world, who have, and continue to impact or touch your life in positive ways. Find as many ways, large and small, as you can to let them know what they mean to you. Keep them close in heart and spirit and pray for them often. Let go of those who are not willing to see you as God see's you.

Recognize that there is a season for every facet of your life and that, at some point you will need to bring those who help you stay on purpose closer to you and release the rest.

Think about the people you count on to be there for you—imagine how you would feel or function without them.

If you are serious about being unstoppable in life, you must be present to the blessings that continue fill your life. Seek to live your divinely purpose driven life and when you know who you are and whose you are—Act like it!

# Chapter 5

## Searching for a Mentor or Still Searching for Dad?

> He said to me, *"My **grace** is sufficient for you, for my strength is made perfect in weakness.* Therefore most gladly I will rather boast in my infirmities, that the power of Christ may rest upon me.

> *2 Corinthians 12: 9*

**Word Wealth: grace.** From the same root as *chara*, "joy"and *chairo* "to rejoice". It is the word for God's grace as extended to sinful man. It signifies unmerited favor, undeserved blessings, a free gift.

*After all this time, you'd think I would know the difference. Yet, every time I thought I had met the person who would mentor me into my mission in life, they would go away. It never worked out and I was truly confused. I did not understand why God hadn't put that person in my life to mentor me, guide me and watch over me and . . . Oh, sound familiar . . . Things came to light when a friend of mine suggested that maybe instead of searching for a mentor; I was really searching for Dad. Whoa! What a thought!*

I have always been struck by the power that words have to move people, to laughter or to tears, to declare good intentions or to totally deny any involvement in whatever is going on. Most importantly, words from the heart have to power to either break your spirit or to lift you to a place where you believe that anything is possible.

## *We don't know until we know, so get over it!*

I've always *had* what I needed—I just didn't always know it. Just as Angela Burt-Murray, past Editor-in-Chief of Essence magazine wrote, "I decided to focus on the positive by making a list of how **God had touched me with His favor."** Those words resonated in me as I wondered how best to acknowledge all that God has brought me through (not just this year), as well as, give thanks in joyful anticipation for all that is yet to come.

The truth is, we don't all feel the same—about ourselves; our life choices; or our feelings about how or whether we have been touched by God's favor. It's now always clear as some would like to think. I understand how our past & present situations (sometimes called trials & tribulations) greatly impact our world view and dictate how we see ourselves in the world. And that's the set-up—because everything that we see goes through our own **life funnel,** if you will, allowing us to feel God's favor or not—to feel His touch or not—and to believe or not, that God wants to give you the desires of you heart.

While some might believe, based on what has happened in their lives, that "life is out to get them" and they have no control over anything, others believe that "someone" is looking out for them and if they "do the right thing" everything will be okay. Conversely, there are people who have been broken in body and spirit and are lost—their life funnel blocked by disappointment and feelings of failure, as well as, those who always seem to see the light at the end of the tunnel.

I know that **God has touched me with His favor**—I have the situations (case studies), the evidence and the proven results—which have continually met and exceeded expectations.

Here are just a few:

## *Favor of Family Legacy*

**Stopped:** My grandparents worked as sharecroppers in Arkansas in the 1900's; faced racism, poverty, limited resources, hatred and the evil consequence of discrimination. In the introduction, I gave you a glimpse of the challenges they had to face. And showed you how, against all odds, they laid the foundation for their children—to live a better life, to prosper and to have a positive impact on society. It was not important that they might not live to see those seeds sprout up in the lives of their children, or even their grandchildren. My grandparents planted the seeds and left the rest to God.

**Unstoppable:** In spite of all that was going on around them, they planted seeds of hard work, education, faith (fellowship), and family values. Their minds and hearts were focused on their God-given mission and they accepted it and did what they had to do.

A few sprouts from those seeds:

- When my Uncle Charles graduated from the 8th grade, he decided that he wanted to continue his education. Remember that this was the 1900's in Arkansas where *"the amount of land allocated to the sharecropper was determined by the number of productive laborers within the family"*. My Uncle was considered a productive laborer.

  But, he had made up his mind. So, he told his parents that he was going to Little Rock to enroll, in the nearest school for black children, Dunbar High School. And because my grandparents believed in the power of education, he was allowed to go.

  So, my Uncle made his own bicycle, gathered his things, and headed out in pursuit of his goals. When he was just outside of Boydell, Arkansas, his bike broke down. And as he was trying to figure out how to fix it, the landowner (who owned the land his family lived on) came by in his truck and stopped. And the conversation went something like this:

**Owner:** Aren't you one of those Diggs boys?

**Uncle Charles:** Yes, sir (he was always very polite)

**Owner:** Where are you going with your things and your bike?

**Uncle Charles:** I'm going to Little Rock. I'm going to go to High school to further my education.

The landowner sat looking at him and pondering the situation. He asked about the bike and my Uncle told him it had broken down. After a while:

**Owner:** Get your bike, put it in the back and get in the front seat with me.

*Not only was it unheard of for a landlord to allow one of his workers to leave the farm—it was an impossibility to imagine a black person riding in the front seat with a white person. My mom and I were talking about it and she said it was like an angel was watching out for her brother. (Pause to think about that)*

My Uncle Charles didn't have any plans or a place to stay in Little Rock. His only goal was to register for school. So, he found part-time work and a place to stay in back of a lady's house (whom he just met). The next day, he went to Dunbar High and was told that he couldn't register because he wasn't a resident. With that same determined spirit, Uncle Charles, returned to school day after day, hoping to register so that he could continue his education.

One day the Principal came out and asked him what he was doing. After telling his story, the Principal just looked at him, as if pondering the situation and told him to go inside and register for school. My Uncle Charles graduated from Dunbar High School, went on to further his education, served in World War II and returned to the same school as a Science teacher. **Favor.**

- I've mentioned what the presence of my Aunt Wilma has meant to my life. Of how she knew that she was loved without measure and carried that joyful spirit with her right up to the end of her life. I would always say I want to be just like my Aunt Wilma.

  One time, when she was in San Diego, I took her to the grocery store with me. She was in her nineties then. As I shopped, rather than have her walk around too much, I told her to stay by the basket while I walked over to get the grocery items. I turned to walk away and as soon as I got where I was going, I noticed out of the corner of my eye, someone coming straight toward me. As I turned, I realized it was my Aunt and that in that instant, she had charged over to where I was. All I could do was smile and for the rest of the shopping trip, we walked together. **Blessing.**

- Our family is blessed to continue to celebrate new life. From the families of the many cousins and young people who continue to carry our family legacy of love. To the children of my brother who welcomed two precious sons, his grandsons, into the world in January and June of the same year that he left us. **Love.**

## *Favor in Living Space*

**Stopped:** After years spent funding my dreams, the resources available to me seemed to dry up. I was left with a shortfall and the subsequent loss of my home. I had finally bought a home, all by myself! And I lost it! Shame! Where do I go from here? (Oh, did I mention being in a car accident that totaled my car, as well.)

**Unstoppable:** I let go and I let God. I held on to what I had accomplished so far and I let go of the loss. I held on to the God's unfailing hand and I let go of the shame. I held on to my dreams and allowed God to lighten my load. I trusted that what I didn't know, God did. And I moved on.

Oh, about the car accident—there were witnesses on the scene who saw the whole thing. They reported that it was not my fault at all and that the other car hit me (my head was a little fuzzy at the time). The paramedic and the fire department were on the scene immediately. My car had turned upside down and when it stopped (before going off an embankment), I has been rolled over and around so that I was hanging by the seat belt, inside the car between the front and back seat facing the trunk. I was upside down—still wearing my glasses and shoes and I could see oncoming traffic. I know for a fact that God can stop traffic. I must have closed my eyes because I remember opening them looking out the back window and just before that *I felt my angels roll me over inside the car. (That's my truth and I'm sticking to it)*

## Favor in Business

**Stopped:** Feeling stuck—praying for clarity and expansion—I shifted gears and went to *work* as a Security Guard to pay the bills. Actually, I enjoyed the experience a lot. I worked in a variety of outdoor and indoor events and met some great people. It was fun for a while. But, as God knew, I had to get back to my own business.

**Unstoppable:** I was on the computer and saw a teleseminar titled, "Everything You Wanted to Know About Working for Seminar Companies" so I signed up. Based on the information shared in the teleseminar, I selected and contacted the seminar company that I wanted to work with. The time that I planned to audition was delayed because of the car accident. So, when I finally called to set an appointment, I was told that if I waited a few more weeks, auditions would be held in San Diego. That meant that I wouldn't have to travel (and pay for it myself) to the home office located out of town. **Yeah! Favor!**

Subsequently, I was offered a contract and my new journey began. As a contract Trainer, my world was expanded. I had the opportunity to travel to places where I hadn't been before, including Hawaii and Alaska. It became clear to me that my presentation and speaking style was more than enough. In fact, I discovered the magic of being, not just presenting. The magic of being in the moment—receiving gems of wisdom that come when I get out of my own way and focus on what I am here to give.

## *Favor in Friendship*

**Stopped:** One of my pet peeves is when someone tries to interpret the meaning behind my words or the intention behind my actions. I don't know about you, but that just works every nerve in my body. I think to myself (or say it out loud), **you don't know me, who the h—do you think you are!** It appalls me when someone thinks they know what is in my heart better than I do. I am not talking about people who see something in me that I don't see (either positive or negative) and point it out with kindness or even directness in wanting to help me to be a better person. I'm talking about people who don't see or acknowledge how I have changed and hold on to *who I used to be*. As if that was all to the story and it were a done deal! You know who they are. And every time you allow them to comment on the person God is re-creating you to be, you are reminded of everything that is wrong with you and you are diminished.

**Unstoppable:** I have friends who listen to me with a loving heart as I share my deepest fears, vulnerabilities and my dreams. They remind me of the gifts that I have been given, encourage me to keep moving forward and care enough to tell me the truth, just as I need to hear it. They have taken the time to get to know me and they know how to speak to and approach me to get the best out of me.

You see, my life funnel has helped to bring me to a place of wonder and pure joy in knowing that I am in good hands, and always have been. My faith in the journey allows me to look forward in gratitude and joy, trusting that I am on the right path. And the greatest shift for me has been in the realization that in order to get to this place, I had to allow myself to be teachable from the inside out. What a concept!

It continues to amaze me how a simple question or statement or observation can prompt us to see things a different way, or in a way that we never imagined before. Oftentimes it depends on the messenger. In some cases we may ask, do I know, trust or even like this person? In other cases, it we are open to receive the message; it can come from a stranger, a good movie, or even from someone we don't like. So when my friend lovingly suggested that instead of searching for a mentor, I might be searching for my Dad (still?), I must have been in a teachable moment, because it made sense to me and I got it right away.

In my mind, a mentor is someone who knows more than I do and agrees to provide a safe place to exchange thoughts and ideas. A mentor is willing to share their wisdom with me; to help me avoid some of the pitfalls in life and to assure me that we can work through problems together. Oh, and that person also has my back when I need them to (does this sound familiar).

As I thought about it, I have had mentors all throughout my life. At different times with different people who, all the while, were under the guidance, grace and favor of God. Bottom line, it was time for **me** to do something. I didn't need to search for anything or anyone. I had all that I needed.

**Food for thought:** Imagine for a moment what your life would be like if you stopped *searching* for that thing that seems to be just out of reach. It could be a new car, a home, money, a dream vacation, or even that **right** relationship. What if you took the thing you are most passionate about and spent some time figuring out ways you can be of service? You know the suggestion in my introduction about giving away the very thing that you need. Because what we do know; is that is takes energy to resist the things in life we don't like or to spend time *wishing* life was different, and in the end, all you get is a headache and maybe some heartache. It doesn't change a thing.

Imagine what you can do if you take that same level of energy and intensity, and focus on ways that your life can be expanded in order to help those who can't help themselves. Wouldn't it be great if more people could feel God's favor and blessings in their lives through your actions? Life presents plenty of opportunities to *shift* our thinking, just slightly, away from "what's in it for me", to "how can I help you". By shifting our thoughts we are reminded that we already have what we need inside of us. Then we can see that when we give something away to help another person, we actually expand our own spiritual connection. I don't mean giving to the point where our own energy and resources have been depleted—that would defeat the purpose.

What I am suggesting is that when you get it! When you understand how valuable you truly are in God's eyes; instead of fighting your circumstances, allow your life to be used. Show up just as you are and know that whatever you need is already in place.

## *Starting today*

Reflect on the words of Paul in Galatians 2:20, "I have been crucified with Christ; it is no longer I who live, but Christ lives in me; and the *life* which I now live in the flesh I live by faith in the Son of God, who loved me and gave Himself for me." Think about how your life has changed or evolved over time, without you having to do anything. How many times, can you remember, that you came close to having an accident, or was at the right place at the right time, or witnessed a miracle in the lives of your family, friends and even yourself.

Check out the amount of time you spend searching for, asking about and getting on other peoples nerves (they won't tell you, but I will) by talking about something that you want and don't yet have. Imagine putting that time and energy to work in areas of need in the world. We know for sure that many are in need; in our neighborhoods, churches, on the street, in the workplace, in the community and even in our own homes.

There is an endless supply of need in the world and when you check yourself, using God's words, you will understand that you have an endless supply of resources, as well.

# Chapter 6

## Say What You Mean, Mean What You Say and Stick to It!

*"But others fell on good ground, sprang up, and yielded
a crop a hundredfold."* When He had said these things
He cried. *"He who has ears to hear, let him hear!"*
*Now the parable is this: The seed is the word of God*

*Luke 8:8, 11*

I was reading an article in a magazine about what women need to know about men. I have read several articles like this before, but, this interviewer asked the men a rather profound question. The question was, "do women make you court them?" and the resounding answer from the men was "no". Now it doesn't matter to me what magazine it was in or who the men were, I know the truth when I hear it.

At 60 years young, I had been out of the dating game for some time. I got tired of spiraling in the pool of insanity—doing the same thing expecting different results, so I gave myself a time-out. *It just lasted longer than I expected it to.* During that time, I realized that some of the problems I had in previous relationships were directly related to *my issues.* Okay, I said it! Anyway, since my life on the outside was not getting better in that area, I decided to go underground—to *check myself* on the inside. In my speaking and training engagements, I like to tell to my audience members to "check yourself—before somebody else does—because you know they will". Well, I had been *checked*. And it was time to take care of me.

So, I took the time to get to know me. And I became an observer.

## Stopped

I knew where I was—emotionally I was three years old. My ability to express the deepest feelings inside of me was equivalent to what you might hear from a three year old child. I could repeat some of the words I had heard, but I didn't know how to connect those words to what I was feeling on the inside. On the outside, I could do what it took to survive in the world. I excelled at specific skills and knew how to get ahead in life. I had successfully raised a family and did whatever it took to take care of my loved ones. I was easy to be around, most of the time, and I didn't ask for much. I understood that the small things were most important and in that regard, I was thoughtful, kind and caring.

I was also mad as hell! Even when I made attempts to show my friends how fragile I was inside—emotionally and in relationships with men—they weren't having it. I looked too confident, too put together, too strong and what I found out is that most people believe what they see—or what you allow them to.

To be honest, I wasn't sure how or what I needed to do to show people, especially men, that I **did need** them. I thought that in order to have a man truly love me, I was supposed to **need** a man. Yet, the parts of me that needed to be loved by a man were not visible. They were hidden underneath the pain and fear of what to me, was the unknown.

## Unstoppable

I do believe that when God closes one door, He opens another. When the door to my Dad was closed, the door to my son was opened. Although it was many years later, Gods know when we are ready to receive what he wants to give us. I had actually written down on my list of goals (I was writing down goals before it was popular) that I wanted to have a son by the time I was thirty. And I did! It actually scared the crap out of me. Thinking back, it could have been another one of those times when *intention* met *a made up mind* and was ignited by the *grace of God?* I don't even know. I just know it scared me! And, as a result, I stopped writing down my goals for a period to time.

This was another time in my life when I thought, now what?

So, instead of trying to figure it out, I thought it best to focus on 3 specific lessons that I have learned along the way. These stories come to you courtesy of my daughter, my son and through the *amazing* Grace of God.

## Men are People Too!

**First**—My children are my total opposite when it comes to sharing how they feel. They could tell me how they feel about a situation or event in 0.3 seconds—where it would take me days to get in touch with my inner voice. It was important to me, that they learn how to express themselves effectively.

My daughter is a beautiful woman who can walk into a crowd of men—whether she was in jeans or a body fitting dress—and just be. In fact, it was something I read on an evaluation from one of her professors that struck me. He said, "Trina is comfortable in her own skin". I had no idea what that meant. So, one day I asked her how she did it. She said simply "men are just people". My immediate thought was "really"? Until that moment, I hadn't seen it—I didn't see men as people. As odd as that may sound, it was true.

Again, our imagination is powerful. And my imagination had told me that my Dad (and all other men) weren't real people, like me. They instead, were elusive beings that had a certain power and they lived in a different place that I didn't have access to. It didn't have to make sense. We all make up stories to support our choices and the reasons for our decisions, don't we? So, the first challenge for me was to learn how to see men as people.

I started to observe how women who had healthy relationships with men behaved. I noticed that they seemed to *like* the man in their life. I had loved men, I didn't necessarily like them. Actually, when I think about it, I probably didn't like myself then either (just a thought). When I talked to men, I started to listen to how they expressed themselves and hear what was important to them. It was no longer personal because I was now an observer. I listened to men share their dreams and goals, and bits and pieces of their lives with me. Particularly, the young men, who were friends of my son—I was like another mom to them. They shared with me things they hadn't told their own mothers.

Through these young men I began to see the pain they felt at not having access to a mother or father they could count on. In my neighborhood I was the mean lady, I thought, because I was always outside getting after them (they were ages 7-12) for playing in my yard, or fighting or using inappropriate language. What I found out is, the way they saw it, I cared. I brought them into my home and hosted movie night and took them aside to share tips on how to conduct themselves, in life and in business. I invited them to my annual Kwanzaa celebration and gave them each books to take home with them.

My great-niece was at my home one day, when one of the boys came to the door to ask what I was doing and to talk for a minute. She asked me, Auntie Patrice, do they come over just to talk to you? I answered yes, and she said, boys don't do that—to which I replied, my boys do. That's what they felt like to me—my boys.

I found that some of the older ones hadn't traveled outside of their neighborhoods and those of their relatives. As a result, their world view was limited to the places where they lived. Many had no idea what was possible for them. My desire was to give them a larger view of the world and so I offered them books and encouraged them to venture out of their comfort zones. I think they changed me, more than I changed them.

A new story was forming for me—and I began to slowly see men as people. I began to like and accept them—just as they are. And with that, another piece of my heart was shifted.

## What Comes Around Goes Around . . .

**Second**—The realization that I had a son—a 6'1" man-child growing before my eyes came to me gradually. I believe it happened while I was watching my young son grow up—I was focused on that, so I wasn't paying attention to anything else. And the thing that scared me the most appeared to sneak up on me.

I thought it was life's way of throwing me a curve ball or just messing with me, and then I remembered—I asked for this (I even listed it on my goals). And now I was the one who had been *assigned* to help my son. Of all people, at that time, I thought I was the last person who could handle that task. Has that ever happened to you? Has life ever presented challenges for you to overcome and you were sure they had the wrong person? So, there I was.

At first, I kept doing what I had always done, which is, to control by intimidation—at 5'1" I knew how to get the advantage. I knew that it was important to show the same level of confidence and boldness I had always shown as his mom. And that worked—for a minute. Until one day he looked at me and said (he'd actually said it several times before I got it) "you always have to be right!"—to which I immediately responded, **I do not!** (I think I was five years old emotionally at that time).

After a while, I began to wonder, to myself, could *he* be right? I'd go into my room so he couldn't see my face and go back over our conversation in my mind. I tried to be as accurate as I could and when I took the emotion out of the conversation—it sort of appeared that I may, at times, have had the tendency, to want to appear on the surface, to want to be a little right. OKAY—he as right! I had spent so much time demanding, commanding, and talking at him that I wasn't *listening* to him. And only after I was in the safety and quiet of my bedroom, was I able to admit that I was wrong about something.

Then the strangest thing happened—the weight of always *having* to be right—lifted. I no longer pretended to have all the answers and I started to listen to his point of view. He is actually quite brilliant. Our conversations and exchanges were lighter and we laughed more together. Was this the same son with the mental challenges, of course it was, I only have one son. However, how often do we forget that we are much more our circumstances? That regardless of all the stuff we see on the outside; we have genius, creativity and the brilliance within us to help change the world. And I knew that God was giving me the opportunity to take a Master Class and that my son was the teacher.

## Getting Ready For Love

**Third**—Now what **is** the difference between *needing* a man and *wanting* a man? I've seen women on television proclaim to the world, "I don't need a man". I've heard women say, "I don't need a man, but I want one". According the Webster's dictionary—the word **need** means: lack of something required or desired. The word **want** means: to lack, to crave, to desire—something needed. Hmm—Now I'm really confused. I think we need a new word.

I once heard a preacher on the radio say that women ought to make sure that their man can bring something to their relationship that elevates her and makes her life better in some way—before she marries him. I liked that. Well, it made sense to me. Anyway, I needed to get back to my own quest to deal with my *issues,* first.

I had to ask myself, what does God require of me, as a woman? So, I went to Proverbs 31, because this was not a standard that was set by men, it was a high standard for womanhood, set by a woman, who had walked the talk. Proverbs 31:10-28, gives a pretty detailed description of what it takes to be a virtuous woman. It almost appears that she has to be superwoman to qualify. Remember that this is a high standard, and as such, covers all possible scenarios from all aspects of life. I don't believe that we are required to be all things in all situations—that place is reserved for God. However, I do believe we are required to use this as a guide and to become the best woman we can be—with the right intention, a made-up mind in our commitment to Christ, and to be teachable, so that when God speaks to us—we are able to hear.

Now, one thing I know for sure is that I am constantly in process. Meaning I am still and forever will be—learning. I do believe that God has requirements of me as a woman and that He wants me to be: trustworthy, happy, prosperous, smart, wise, confident in my value, kind, considerate, business-minded, blessed, and to carry myself in a way that the man in my life will want to praise me. And that was good, but, I thought, how do I know when those things have been accomplished in my life?. Would I get a seal of approval for all to see?

I found that when I stop *trying* to be who God wants me to be and I relax and rely on Him to teach me, I don't have to think about it. The word *trying* is an interesting word. In some languages, there is no translation for it. There are only two points of view. You are either doing something or you are not. It either *is or it isn't*—there is nothing in-between. So, for me, I was either going to rely on God to mold me or not. There was no other way to look at it.

## Food for thought

I was having a conversation with a male friend and we were talking about relationships. He told me that when he grew up, in the South, men wouldn't dare do the stuff they were doing today. He said that the women would put them on lockdown real fast, because they were raised to expect more from their men. They expected men to court them—and that was not up for debate. So, when I read the question in the article asking men if they had to court women in order to get next to them, I thought about that. And since I am starting over, so to speak, I thought this is the perfect time for me to find out what I mean, to mean it when I say it and to be able to stick to it!

Over the past year, I have had the honor to observe a healthy relationship between a girlfriend of mine and her man. It has been a privilege to see from the inside, what it takes to sustain a respectful, loving, caring, healthy relationship from their perspective. At times, it scared me because I wasn't sure if I could be patient enough or put away sarcasm and cynicism so that I could do my part in a healthy relationship.

The great thing about having a sneak peek into their relationship has been getting a chance to see it in slow motion; just as it was happening. For some reason, I always felt a relationship had to go fast. I didn't necessarily want it like that, but I didn't know how to change my behavior. Seeing them interact in a step-by-step, day to day, event by event basis allowed me to see them grow and evolve over time, as individuals and as a couple. It helped me to see that a good relationship doesn't happen overnight. From the inside view, I could see that just like other things in my life, developing a good relationship with someone special was a process. As I was familiar with going through processes, my fear of the unknown began to fade, sort of. But, either way, I knew a blessing when I saw one.

As a strategic thinker, I realized that I had to determine what would work for me—as far as dating is concerned. Based on the fact that I have taken the time to do the work—to deal with what had me stopped, I know that I am exactly who God wants me to be. I know that, in this moment, I am enough. That being said, I thought about what the preacher on the radio had said about women choosing a man who could elevate her and make her life better in some way. Contrary to what you may think, that does not always mean buying us things or giving us money—although that is quite acceptable.

## Been there

As I thought more about it, I recalled that I **had** been in a relationship where I felt like a virtuous woman. I remember the feeling. It was years ago, when my son was nine or ten years old. I had run into a friend from school and we started dating. The funny thing is that over the years I had been thinking about him and wondered how he was doing.

He was, and probably still is, an athletic person, so working out was a part of his life. We would meet at the park to walk and use the slant board to do sit ups and he made it fun and easy. It didn't feel like work to me and I must say that I felt like I was in the best shape of my life. We went out to dinner, attended church and spent time with friends and family together. I was being courted—and it felt good.

It was further confirmed, when my son looked up at me (he was still looking up at me then) and said, Mom, he's good for you. I just looked at him speechless. I knew that his comments were not based on what this man did for him or for me (although he had done things for us), or how much stuff he had. My son's observation was based upon the changes he had seen in me. In how he had seen my spirit being elevated as a direct result of the glow I felt in being treated like woman—who was praised by her man. This man had a good job, a Christian family, and his own strategy for handling the challenges placed in his life. He didn't need me to develop one for him. Yes, he was good for me and I will never forget him. But, the deal is our lives were going in different directions and I loved him (and liked him) enough to wish him the best in taking his life where God wanted him to go.

Even today, when I think about that relationship, I can smile, because I know I didn't miss out on anything. We gave the best of what we had to offer to one another, at that time—what more can you ask?

## Starting today

What will it take for you to feel like a virtuous woman by your man? What would your life look like if you chose to look within, face your issues and do the work needed to become the person God wants you to be? Whether it prepares you to be in a successful relationship or not is up to you. However, when you make the decision to walk closely with God, your issues will be revealed.

Just as you decide the kind of home, car, lifestyle, vacation and goals you want to achieve in life, you also choose the people you allow into your life. At least, I hope you do. If not, you may be wondering why the same type of people keep showing up.

So, ladies, if you decide that a healthy relationship is for you, I have a couple of questions. Would you be ready if 'Mr. Right in God's light' showed up in your life? Or would you have to start bargaining with God for more time to get ready? And then hope you have the time that you need.

I know this: when you show up as trustworthy, happy, prosperous, smart, wise, confident, kind, considerate, and taking care of business woman, it is easier to open your heart to the man who will be proud to treat you as his virtuous woman. You just have to make sure you know what you really want.

## Bonus story: A man in the making

On June 2, 2011, I attended my great-niece's graduation ceremony. She and five other classmates were graduating from Headstart. It was a lot of fun to see them dancing, singing, and reciting what they had learned together as their teacher interacted with them. During the ceremony, I noticed one young boy who I felt stood out from the rest. He had on black slacks, a white shirt, nicely cut hair (he wore it long) and had an air of confidence. In fact, after the diplomas were given out, his mom said that he wanted to speak to the class. She didn't know what he was going to say—he told her he would just wing it. (Okay!). He then addressed his teachers and eloquently told them what he had learned from them and how much he *appreciated* all that they had done for him. Well, he had my vote.

After the ceremony, his mother came over to tell us something else her son had said. She spoke in Spanish to our close family friend. Evidently, he told his mom he was going to go to school, graduate from college, become an astronaut, buy his mother a house, find my great—niece, fall in love and marry her. This is Headstart! They aren't even in Kindergarten yet. I must also add that my great-niece had two other beaus vying for her attention. One of them gave her a rose (her first) a real one!

*So, what were this young man's attributes?*

He was confident, consistent, looked good and stood out from the rest. He had already proven he could make a commitment and stick with it and he has a plan for the future. This plan included getting his education, following a career path, taking care of his Mom and *then,* when he had done all that, he would find the woman of his dreams, fall in love & marry her. I think I'm in love.

Are we to expect less from the man we give our love to? I'm just saying . . .

# Chapter 7

## Are You Unstoppable Yet?

But those who **wait** on the Lord shall renew *their* strength;
They shall mount up with wings like eagles, They shall run
and not be weary, They shall walk and not *faint.*

*Isaiah 40:31*

I love this scripture! To me, it contains, when all is said and done, the most important thing that we must do, in order to allow God's light to shine through us. That would be to **wait**. The word means to remain (until something expected happens), to be ready, act or a period of waiting, to act as a servant, to serve.

That does not mean waiting is fun or easy to do. I wasn't good at it because I wanted to get to the action. You see, I wanted to know exactly what had to be done to keep things moving forward. During times of calm and stagnation (I called it), when everything was still, I was uncomfortable. So, rather than accept and enjoy the moments of peace, I would *do* something to shake things up.

My life has always been filled with dips, valleys, highs and lows; like being on a constant roller coaster. So, I had come to expect it. I thought moving forward was my middle name. It may be that I felt like you couldn't hit a moving target or it helped me to ignore what was missing in my life. Whatever it was, being still was something that I had to learn to do—to be.

## *Unstoppable*

The word *unstoppable* means to remove the stopper from or to clear an obstruction. A stopper is used to hold something in or to keep other things out. An obstruction could be an event, or situation or *issue* that is either holding us in place or keeping us from moving. Either way, to unstop something can be a good thing. Once an obstruction is cleared, for example, all the good things and blessing just waiting to enter your life can flow freely. Imagine how good your life can become if you removed all the stoppers.

On the other hand, if the floodgate of blessings were to open into your life without any filter, guidelines or instruction on how to handle them, you may drown. We've seen it time and time again, someone gets a windfall—wins the lottery—and before long, without wise counsel or direction, they are worse off than they were before. So, waiting becomes crucial. And, just because we manage to remove one obstruction doesn't mean there won't be more. When we finally manage to remove one stopper, we usually find out that we have other places that have been plugged up in our lives. Most often, we don't even know where the stoppers are located, until we get there.

Then we have a relapse. We fall back. Not necessarily to where we began, but, we fall back nonetheless. There are no skip-overs. If you miss a lesson or overlook something that you need to know, you will be put in check. You will have another opportunity to get the lesson again, and again, until you get it! Then you can move on to the next one. After a while, the momentum of your life will begin to speed up and with practice, patience and trust, your lessons will become easier to see.

## *Mount up with wings like eagles*

The truth is that not everyone wants to mount up with wings like eagles—there are those who would rather work behind the scenes and that's cool—everyone has a part. Yet, those who choose to find a way to soar are often the targets of those who choose not to. A difference in perspectives, experiences, beliefs and perceptions, about *how* a godly person ought to mount up always creates cause for debate. It is similar to the debate about money being the root of all evil. Conversations get heated, friends fall out, even godly people act ugly all under the guise of interpreting the word of God.

The most important work you will have to do is to allow God to get on the inside. Only He can soften those hard places (where the soil is bad), and replace the seeds of pain with joy, hate with love, and anger with compassion. We can't do it by ourselves because, as humans, we allow fear to stop us, anger to paralyze us and the 'lack' in our lives to place us in danger. After all, we have plenty of *stuff* to keep us distracted, don't we?

Does it seem like just when you decide that you are going to mount up and soar, something happens to either stall you or shut you down? Or do people you count on to support you and encourage you suddenly become silent or go away? The truth is, we don't know what is behind every door or see the intention in every lesson and for that, we have to wait on God to reveal it to us. For example, if you decide to start your own business, you must do things that will help you to develop a business mindset.

## Mission mindset

For example, identify a person in business who successfully doing what you want to do. Take the time to observe their character based on the way he or she does business and how they treat other people. Introduce yourself and make contact with the intention of developing a relationship with that person. Remember, that people do business with people they like. Therefore, when you feel there is a mutual respect and trust between you, ask that person to be your mentor. Following this practice will give you an advantage in the learning curve and save you time.

Another tip to help you be successful in any goal you want to achieve is to first, have a base line for determining good character. I was watching a program on television and one person was going to give another person a lie detector test, but, first he had to establish a base line. I like that—if you don't have a way to recognize a lie, how do you know it's a lie. I had learned to detect a lie in my children and even in my granddaughter because I had a base line. I know the difference between a lie and the truth when I see it on their face and hear it in their voice. However, I had to be able to view it from both sides so that I could make the differentiation.

You may ask, what is a base line for good character? I am so glad you asked. In the bible in I Corinthians 13:1-13, Paul explains the absolute necessity of love and gives its characteristics and contrasts in relation to that which is temporary and that which lasts beyond a lifetime. It is the same thing when you need to know if someone's word is only good for today or if it can be counted on to last a lifetime. When you haven't taken the time to get to know yourself, you may believe you are making choices out of love, when in fact you could be operating out of envy and pride. It can happen to anyone.

For example, I love to laugh and have fun. People who are with me when I start to laugh may think I am being downright silly. However, I know that my laughter is directly connected to the joy I feel inside and that in those moments, I am in my most brilliant mind. I have a base line for knowing whether I am a state of showing little sense of judgment or I am in a complete state of joy and rejoicing—no matter what anyone else thinks.

In that same regard, I know what the feelings of envy, pride and jealously *feel* like on the inside. And when those feelings rise up in me, I know that I have more work to do. Just like that—I try to keep it simple.

In my experience, God's word is the only one I have found that never changes. Truth does not change. And when I first, follow the teachings in scripture to help create a base line for good living—I can't go wrong. Particularly since I have decided to run this race and not be weary; I know that God will notify me when I need to rest. I know that when I walk I will not faint because when the going gets tough, He will carry me. As far as I know, there is no other place where you count on that—and get a guarantee.

I am so grateful that I have seen the proof and I know deep in my spirit, that God is mentoring me. I am not alone. I had to learn that and once I did, there was no turning back. Partly, because I can see the places where my life, and the lives of my loved ones, has been protected and saved. The other part is that I have accepted what God has given me to do and I am serious about that. So serious that I can't afford to be distracted by what other people do, say or think—that is none of my business—I have enough to do.

When you make the decision to use your gifts to help other people; and to step into a wider audience, your life will be changed. I heard years ago, that not everyone will be able to go all the way with you. When I first heard it, I was sad. The thought of having to 'leave someone behind' just because I wanted more out of life, felt a little like betrayal. My own experience with feelings of betrayal caused me to be sensitive to others, in that regard. As I began to do the work, on the inside, I found that I didn't have to focus on or worry about who stayed in my life and who didn't. It occurred naturally. I had to be willing to let those go who didn't want to be there, appreciate those who stayed and then choose for myself who I wanted to take forward in my life.

## *Your inner circle*

Who is in your inner circle? Who are the people with whom you share your deepest secrets? Do they encourage you to be all that God wants you to be? Can you tell that they care enough to get to know you on the inside and keep your best interests in mind? Are you confident, by the way they talk to you and respond to you, that they have been paying attention? Or do you spend time constantly defending your actions or trying to convince them that you didn't really lose your mind? Do you feel exhausted or empty after interacting with them? Or after a brief connection, do you feel excited and energized about what the future holds?

Do you feel at home in conversation and in person, with those close to you? Is it safe to cry, scream, laugh, rejoice and just be yourself? Wisdom in action means that you have received the lesson; that you know what you need to do; and that, no matter how you feel about it, you are willing to do what needs to be done, in service to God.

## *Unstoppable*

To be unstoppable does not mean that you are perfect or immune from conflict by any means. To me, it means, that in spite of the fact that you have lost a loved one, or lost your home or you feel depressed and aren't sure if you want to live to see another day, that you realize there is help. And that you are willing to do whatever it takes to get the help you need, by any means necessary, without hurting anyone else. That when you feel life's distractions pulling you away from your dreams and your divinely planned purpose, you will respond in love, get reinforcement from your inner circle and keep on moving forward.

Remember that your story is just that—your story—and that although something has happened *to you*, that event or situation does not define who you are or what you can accomplish in life.

The truth is, no one has the right to impose limitations on your life. You are limited by what you believe about yourself and what is possible and by whom you allow to have an impact on your life.

In this book, I have shared how my life has been impacted by a variety of situations and circumstance, while as the same time, showing you how I have responded in ways that bring me closer to the person I have been designed to be. The path I've had to take was crooked not straight, and I couldn't see what was around the next corner or know whether I would reach my destination or not. I knew this for sure: I wanted to keep going. And for that to be true, I had to have the best, most positive counsel, relationships and attitude.

## *Your inner voice*

I still struggle. There are times that I struggle to identify my true feelings, especially verbally. It is easier for me to write about it. I have always enjoyed writing poems and letters to my friends and loved ones to express how I feel about them. I remember when a friend was leaving town, I had written a poem to express how much she meant to me. I ended up on stage reading it out loud, although that was not my original intention. As I walked back to my seat, a woman known to be very good poet, leaned over and said, you are a poet. I thanked her and kept walking. I didn't think more about it because *I just like to write.*

Another time I was at a business event and a friend walked by, as I was talking to someone else, pointed at me and said, she's a writer. I thought, that's an interesting thing to say. I still didn't see myself as a writer.

When I started to write this book and I was getting feedback from a close friend—I told her how surprised I was at how easily the words were flowing. Her response was, *isn't that something, and you're not even a writer*—then she laughed—okay, I got it!

The interesting thing is I am an intuitive, creative, quick thinking person. With that being said, I don't know everything—not even close. When I started my business, I had the intention of becoming a speaker probably because I was trying to find my inner voice. I found great joy in writing my speeches and found it was easy to do, yet, I didn't make the connection. I put more importance into standing before people and using my voice to make a point or to make a difference. You might say, I had taken the written word for granted.

You see, I could easily recognize the speaker in me. When I wanted to hone and develop my speaking skills I joined Toastmasters. However, I have never thought to join a writing group. I didn't see myself in that way. Only after the truth seemed to haunt and follow me was I able to see the possibility—I am a writer. That is amazing to me.

Can you think of a time when you thought you had the right answer or were convinced you understood clearly what you were to do, and then something else appeared that you hadn't noticed before? Suddenly, you realize it was there all the time and even though you are still hesitant to call it by name, you know the truth when you finally allow yourself see to it. Isn't that the human way? We have the ability to open ourselves to the truth and see what is happening in our lives, or conversely, we can shut down and close our minds to deny what is possible. This capability is unique to us, as human beings.

## Choose to be open

Once I made the choice to be open to what I needed to hear, I immediately knew that I had to have the support of loved ones to help me handle the truth. There is something about facing the truth that can be a bit scary.

As I was going through a dark time in my life, a longtime friend came to me and said, Patrice hold on, help is on the way! Knowing that she is grounded in the word of God gave me solace because I knew what she said was true.

When talking to a beloved friend, who has been with me most of my life, I shared details of a conversation I had with a speaking colleague. She knew I was excited and looking forward to having the conversation. She listened and asked if something the other person said had hurt my feelings. My immediate response was "oh no, he just told me the truth". Afterward, because she has asked the right question, I began to think about it. An hour later (I'm getting better) I called her back and said, "heck yes! It hurt my feelings". We both laughed.

Acknowledging that truth enabled me to move quickly through the emotions of hurt, sadness, anger and then to that tenacious spirit that makes me unstoppable. With her help, I was able to accomplish something in a few hours that would normally have taken a week or longer. *What a blessing.*

## Unconditional Love

I wrote this to express what unconditional love looks like and feels like to me through my relationship with my granddaughter Destiny:

### No One Could Have Told Me Then

When I became a mom, I was but a child you see
So low on self-esteem at seventeen
Not able to imagine the joy that lie ahead
Unaware of the journey called life, some call it destiny
Would hold answers to my life long search for love, for unconditional love
No one could have told me then.

So as I watched my little girl grow and saw my own reflection through her eyes as I strived to make her journey better, better than mine
Felt pretty complete when on the day, mission competed
My little girl grew into that woman and more than I ever imagined, what a joy!
Yet, no one could have told me then.

You see, I no longer searched for that elusive love to fill me up inside and help me to shine from the inside out, that's always been my truth
So, on this day I could not foresee the miracle that lie ahead for me
When my daughter whispered those words in my ear
"Mom, I'm pregnant: she said.
Even then, no one could have told me.

Just after she arrived, I held her in my arms
Embraced her warmth in the nape of my neck
Moved through my body and soothed my soul lifted me to
a higher place, in just one embrace
I can still feel that first time we met
And still, no one could have told me then.

No one could have told me that my life would be changed
in such ways to end my life long search for unconditional
love through the birth of a child called Destiny who chose
to call me "Ma"

No one could have told me then
Had to feel it for myself
Like when she would run and jump into my arms just
because I came through the door
Allowed me to escape to a place in her embrace
Released the trigger holding all of my misguided fears of
blowing the only chance at love I thought I had
Behind the many years of tears

No one could have told me then that in a moment I would
be set free
Free to create a new legacy
Through the eyes of this child called Destiny
My own destiny would unfold
Forever changed, forever love
No one could have told me then.

Copyright 2006—Patrice C. Baker
Published in Sparkle-Tudes Heart of a Mother—by
Sheryl L. Roush

# Chapter 8

## So, What's Next?

*This is the secret of joy. We shall no longer strive for our own way, but commit ourselves, easily and simply, to God's way, acquiesce in His will and in so doing find our peace.*

*Evelyn Underhill*

One of the most profound journeys in my life began with the question, what do I do now? In that case it was because I wanted to help my son. So, it seems appropriate that when one journey appears to end, as we know it, there may be another waiting just around the corner.

In preparation for receiving all God has in store for you, you must first be open to what's next? It doesn't mean you have to know what to do—it does means that you recognize you are not done. So, in all probability you may be called out by life to either check yourself or to be checked once again. And when that happens, it is imperative that you remember what has helped you to get where you are today and embrace the power that you've had inside all along.

You will need to be courageous and committed to letting go of emotions, failures, mistakes and people who cannot support you in the process. The truth is that everyone and everything in your life has helped you to be who you are today. And in the process of letting go, you must be able to use discernment and wisdom.

It doesn't mean that when people disagree with you or disappoint you that you have license to release them. I am not suggesting that you take inventory and based on how you feel in the moment, start kicking people out of your life.

What I am saying is that when you take the time to get to know yourself, embrace your divinely planned purpose and trust God to lead the way, you will be gently and lovingly guided toward your truth.

## *The power of letting go:*

The seeds planted by my grandparents gave sprout to the favor of God and the many blessings in our family. And in the process of letting go of the stuff in my way, I found those sprouts had become doors that opened my life to more than I ever imagined. Just as I believe that when one door closes another one always opens.

**When I let go:** After the loss of my Dad, I felt that something I had been waiting for was stolen from me. Underneath the smile on my face was *anger* that seethed just below the surface. I couldn't allow that anger to be seen because I didn't know if I would be able to control it.

**The door:** After healing the anger the door opened to *genuine joy*. I found out I wasn't the only person filled with anger—I was not alone. Eventually the fear of showing my true feelings faded as I connected with others; sharing my story and listening to theirs. I now understand that my emotions are part of who I am and with balance I will always have access to my joy.

**When I let go:** When I was in elementary school my teacher tape recorded our voices. When I heard my own voice, I remember putting my head down on the table in embarrassment. You see, my voice was nasally (sinus problems) and kind of deep. And even though no one else seemed to notice, I thought I sounded like a boy. It was a *judgment* (one of many) that I carried throughout my life. And I hid it behind a veneer of cynicism and sarcasm.

**The door:** After healing the judgment the door to *compassion* was opened. With compassion my heart opened to a deep trust and sympathy for other people that I had hadn't felt before. I began to see how some of the most innocent situations have caused us to judge ourselves unfairly. It became my goal to assist others in overcoming what they perceived as shortcomings with compassion.

**When I let go:** I was filled with *shame*. If I made a mistake or had an embarrassing moment, the *shame* of it would overcome me. I was ashamed of being so angry and afraid of being found out. I felt shame when I didn't have the right answer to problems or the right response in an awkward conversation. And because I was too ashamed to admit it, I didn't know the difference.

**The door:** In healing the shame the door to *freedom* opened. I began to realize that my shame was more about the amount of effort I put into a particular task, rather than the outcome. And when I did everything I knew to do, in that moment, I was doing my best. With the freedom to be myself and to live without regrets, I was able to move forward with an open heart.

**When I let go:** The one thing we can count on, to be constant in our lives, is *change*. We see it in every aspect of life; from changes in employment, marriage, relationships, careers and even when we change our minds—*change* happens everywhere. However, that doesn't mean we feel good about it. I thought I could avoid the *fear of change* by controlling my environment. Until that day when my life felt so out of control that fear raised its ugly head. I was terrified.

**The door:** Before the fear of change engulfed me, the door to *faith* was opened. I had gotten to the end of the road as I had known it. So, I looked all around me for the answers. I even called my close friends and confidantes. And guess what? None of the answers worked for me and my friends weren't available. In that moment, I realized that I had been looking everywhere but UP!

So, I went through the door of faith. I looked up and prayed to God about it. I cried out my heart to God about it. And, as I have come to know for sure—God has all the right answers to my questions and the remedy for my needs.

**When I let go:** I had built a wall of protection around me to keep me safe, so that no one would ever *abandon* me again. And to make sure, that I wouldn't feel the emptiness of being left alone, I would find a way to leave first.

**The door:** As I healed the anger, judgment, shame and fear of my past—the door to *vulnerability* was slowly opened. You see, without anger I had no reason to hold a grudge; without self-judgment I had no reason to judge others; without shame I had no reason to be embarrassed by failure and without the fear of change I had faith that everything would work out. I could show the most vulnerable parts of myself, knowing that no one had the power to use it against me, unless I allowed them to.

Once those doors were opened for me, I could see that the most powerful seeds planted by my grandparents had helped me become free. I was free to be the best, most powerful, spiritually connected person I could be. And with all that I have gone through, I still have the ability to *love* as if I had never been hurt.

And with that, I hope you always remember:

## This Is Your Time

This is your time, to do what you will
To live your hopes, your dreams, to climb that hill.
To take a step higher, than ever before to face the unknown,
to open your door.
To a whole new world, just waiting for you
I wonder. Do you even have a clue?

This is your time. It is not too late
Just open your mind, and tear down the gate.
To those invisible walls, holding you in
Don't you know that you were made to win!
To win at what you might ask
I think Marianne Williamson and
Nelson Mandela said it best.

When they said, and I quote
*"We were born to manifest the glory of God that is within us*
*It's not just in some of us. It's in everyone*
*And as we let our own light shine*
*We unconsciously give other people*
*permission to do the same".*

This is your time. They are calling your name
And if you take up the challenge
You will be forever changed.
Will you come forward and step up to the plate?
As one songwriter wrote, "it's never too late"
To rekindle and revisit your childhood dreams
And ask yourself, "what does my life really mean?"

This is your time. To do what you will
To live your hopes, your dreams, to climb that hill.
To take a step higher than ever before,
To face your fear to go through your door.
That leads to a future—just waiting for you.
If you check in with your spirit
You will know what to do.